Hear, O Israel!

David Solway

Published by
Mantua Books
Brantford, Ontario
N3T 6J9
Email: Mantua2003@Hotmail.com

Library and Archives Canada Cataloguing in Publication

Solway, David, 1941-

Hear, O Israel! / David Solway.

Includes bibliographical references.

ISBN 978-0-9734065-3-5

1. Antisemitism. 2. Arab-Israeli conflict. 3. Terrorism--Religious aspects--Islam. 4. Islamic fundamentalism. 5. Terrorism--Prevention.

I. Title.

HV6431.S6454 2009 363.325 C2009-905698-4

First Printing, October, 2009

Afterward they will get up
all together, and with a sound of chairs scraping
they will face the narrow exit.
Yehuda Amichai, "Resurrection"

Beat your plowshares into swords, and your pruning hooks
into spears: let the weak say: I am strong.
Book of Joel, 3:10

And the hatchers of deceit know
That this fortification will not be easily vanquished.
Natan Alterman, "The Forward Position"
(tr. Sarah Honig)

Acknowledgement

Portions of the following chapters have appeared from time to time as articles in *Arts & Opinion*, *The Métropolitain, Pajamas Media* and *FrontPageMagazine*.

Table of Contents

for Karin and Hannah

1

We Are All Israeli

When debating the subject of the Middle East and the Israeli-Palestinian conflict, we should remember that no history is pure since it is necessarily made by human beings. As all human beings are complicated mixtures of traits both benign and malign, it follows that the history of any people will be a much-chequered fabric of both good and evil.

The history of the Middle East is no different in this regard, except insofar as it has been subject to a greater degree of obfuscation than is usually the case, and therefore requires a corresponding degree of diligence and application in disambiguating its complexities—which is to say, in clarifying its oversimplifications.

The major form of obscurantism in Middle East analysis is the myth of Israeli malfeasance and Palestinian rectitude, of Israeli guilt and Palestinian innocence, which has now acquired so much momentum that facts are almost useless and truth a frequent casualty before its relentless career. The myth consorts with our penchant for easy solutions to intractable problems and our romantic intoxication with the "noble" underdog, the colonial oppressed and the Third World "freedom fighter," idols to which we bow in misconceived adulation. For in supporting these mau-mauing zealots and cult figures—read "Hamas," read "Hizbullah"—we engineer our own unhappiness.

But it is a large and active sector of our "intellectual elite" whose effect is particularly noxious. Without knowing the laminated history of the region, often without even a tentative grasp of the languages or at least a mastery of the salient texts, and without the slightest apprehension of daily life with bombers or the generational anxiety of living in constant expectation of the next suicide attack and incoming rocket or the experience of constant hatred directed at themselves and their families simply for being who they are, our vocal know-nothings have made a cottage industry of legislating down to Israel while continuing to stigmatize it for every imaginable crime in the book.

Others, presumably more competent, are effectively on the Islamic payroll: scholars, university departments, the textbook publishing industry, media personalities, former diplomats and political officials who profit from the monetary grants, lucrative contracts, and high salaries steered their way. Middle Eastern Studies programs, in particular, are fumetted with Arab money.

The anti-Israeli brief is the case as well for American high schools whose history textbooks pull increasingly toward the Islamic narrative. One popular text, *The World*, refers to Jesus as "a young Palestinian," despite the fact that there was no such creature as a "Palestinian Arab" in 30 C.E. and the Gospels themselves tell us that Jesus was born to a Jewish family. Other texts treat Mohammed as being directly inspired by God, without the slightest qualification, while Moses receives the Ten Commandments from the *Hebrew* God Yahweh. Still others are rife with false claims about Islam as indigenous to Palestine, Israel as a war instigator, Arab nations as peace loving, and Israel as responsible for the refugee camps which were in reality the result of deliberate Arab policy.

This travesty has been meticulously documented in an important new work, *the Trouble with Textbooks: Distorting History and Religion*, by Gary Tobin and Dennis Ybarra, a must-read for anyone concerned about the doctoring of the American syllabus. The history of Israel represented in these textbooks, the authors demonstrate in example after example, "reflects too many elements of the Arab narrative without respect to historical accuracy." But this is only a kind of inset or handsel of a much vaster process, the wave of Judeophobia sweeping across the world under the guise of anti-Israelism.

The vilification of Israel, however, should be set within the framework of our own fear and ignorance—what George Weigel in *The Cube and the Cathedral* has called the "failure of moral reason." Israel is only a reflection of our reluctance to gaze into the mirror of time and trace the lineaments of our own beleaguered condition. For the jaded sensibility, the simplifying lie is far more palatable than the candid recognition of our bewildering historical situation. Intellectual maturity and a careful reading of the geopolitical map would help us to understand that, as Eric Hoffer put it in a famous article for the *Los Angeles Times* in 1968, "as it goes with Israel, so it will go with all of us." For Israel is the West's frontline army in the war against militant Islam, its "forlorn hope" (from the Dutch *verleren hoop*, soldiers placed in the most dangerous position or leading the charge).

Certainly, not until we can arrive at some understanding of the upsurge of Jew-hatred in the West and the red herring of anti-Zionism, whether in the form of public odium and acts of antisemitic vandalism or in the flagrant anti-Israeli drift of the media, the Academy, the Churches and the European polity, will we be in a position to confront our weakness and complicity. Only when we realize that, in adopting the Islamic attitude vis à vis Jews and the Jewish state, we are seeking to conciliate rather than confront the forces arrayed against us—that in buying in, we are selling out. For such capitulation only renders us more vulnerable in the long run.

Today, the irony of our situation is especially apt. The shoe is on the other foot—which turns out to be the same foot. The West is beginning to learn what it feels like to be a Jew, to wait for the next murderous assault to break out, to anticipate the next attack upon its homes and places of business or worship, although it has not yet experienced a conscious revelation. A terrorist attack on New York, Madrid, Moscow, London, Paris, Mumbai or any other city is only a pogrom by another name, kindled by religious hatred, applied to a greater range of targets and involving not just Jews but anyone who happens to fall within its radius of destruction.

The global village has become the new *shtetl*, the next Pale of Settlement, the ghetto behind whose political, economic and civic gates the international community now finds itself exposed to punitive expeditions and sudden devastations. A reconsideration of those celebrated lines from a 1946 poem attributed to Pastor Martin Niemöller would not be amiss in the present circumstances:

> First they came for the communists, and I did not speak out—because I was not a communist;
>
> *Then they came for the socialists, and I did not speak out—because I was not a socialist;*
>
> *Then they came for the trade unionists, and I did not speak out—because I was not a trade unionist;*
>
> *Then they came for the Jews, and I did not speak out—because I was not a Jew;*
>
> *Then they came for me—and there was no one left to speak out for me.*

Yet, instead of recognizing a newfound solidarity with its ancestral victim whom it is coming to resemble, the West has chosen to make him responsible for its own, largely self-inflicted distress. It has been, to use Phyllis Chesler's word, "Palestinianized." It has not understood that the Jew is neither provocation nor scapegoat. His presence is not the cause of our troubles and his disappearance is not the answer to our problems. Today especially, he represents precisely both our dilemma and our future.

After the 1980 bombing of a Paris synagogue which killed four people, French Prime Minister Raymond Barre condemned "a despicable act that sought to target Jews…and which struck innocent Frenchmen…" *Gevalt*, such a mistake! Succumbing to a frivolous distinction, Monsieur Barre did not draw the appropriate conclusions then and neither have we today. The popular slogans propagated by the myrmidons of the Left, the "Israel Apartheid" mongers and the "peace" marchers of our time—"We are all Hamas" and "We are all Hizbullah"—are no less quaint than they are suicidal. The fact is, whether we know it or not, we are all Jews now. And we are all Israeli.

2

The Darkness of Antisemitism

Hatred of the Jew, wrote Max Nordeau in *The Conventional Lies of our Civilization* (1884), is a symptom of the degeneration of the national spirit and character, and this is as true now as it was when Nordeau penned these words.

Antisemitism is the public expression of the underlying irrationality that brings the great civilizing project of the West into serious question, from the time of the Greeks and the Romans through the advent and diffusion of Christianity to the present importation of Islamic Jew-hatred into the Western cultural matrix. It is the way in which we turn against ourselves, the pagan residue of acrimony against what poet A. M. Klein called the annunciation of "the world's first fidelity." A deep resentment continues to seethe against Judaism's bequest to mankind: a God who is One, the concept of a universal moral law and the principle of transcendent justice, the exercise of skeptical inquiry into the claims of arbitrary authority, and the importance of individual choice and judgment in taking responsibility for personal salvation.

I would not hesitate to say that antisemitism is the social and intellectual tumour of Western civilization caused in large part (though not only) by the doctrinal and ideological diet prescribed by the early and medieval Christian Church, a malignant growth we have not completely excised. For with the "conversion" of Constantine the Church merely carried on with a vengeance where the pagan Greeks and Romans left off. Even today, the Orthodox Churches refer in their Easter liturgy to Jews as "God-killers" and supplicate, "Repay them, Oh Lord." And the Vatican authorized the revival of the Tridentine Mass, which originally referred to Jews as "perfidious" and portrayed them as living in "darkness." (Despite a papal modification, it still retains a prayer for their conversion.) The latter is by no means as destructive as the former but its revival in the midst of a worldwide antisemitic movement is surely perplexing.

Hatred of the Jew is the perpetual vestige of Western resentment and vexation against its own civilizing imperative. This too was Winston Churchill's understanding of Jew-hatred, which he described as Western civilization's revolt against its own central values as manifested in art, science and political and religious institutions. It is no exaggeration to say that the Jew is the test case of a civilization—a test we appear to have failed. The spectacle we are observing today—the reluctance to deal adequately with terrorism, the political contriving against our own best interests, the serpentine efforts to exculpate the enemy, the relativizing of moral principle, the Left's betrayal of its own liberal culture, the renewed "treason of the intellectuals," and especially the mounting acerbity toward Jews in the court of public opinion and the isolation of Israel as a pariah state—is merely the modern instantiation of this long offensive against our very survival.

We should not be overly surprised at the apparent paradox. If Freud was right in claiming that the individual seeks his or her own path to the grave, so we might say that each civilization arranges its own death.[1] Antisemitism might then be read as the sign of our antinomian destiny as we contend against the terms and demands of our cultural patrimony and continue to anathematize our unacknowledged effigy, passing over our true antagonist. One obvious reason that the Islamic threat is not taken as seriously as it should is that it chimes so harmoniously with the growing strain of antisemitism in the West: the jihadists, the leftward intelligentsia and a considerable stratum of public opinion have made common cause with one another. Additionally, there is also a feeling among more people than we might suspect that, with regard to those we call Islamists, *we are really on the same side*. This is certainly true of Western Europe where, as Bruce Bawer writes in *While Europe Slept*, "the multicultural elite [is], almost without exception, allied with the Islamic right…"

Pascal Bruckner, in his recently published *La tyrannie de la pénitence*, has added a psychological twist to Europe's hostility toward Israel and Jews, viewing it as an attempt to excuse its complicity with or passivity before Hitler's Final Solution: if the Jewish state can be "proven" to be no different from or even worse than the Third Reich, then Europe is off the moral hook. Such an attitude exemplifies the classic operation of psychological projection, that is, in the words of Peter Gay from his *Freud: A Life for Our Times*, the absolution technique "of expelling feelings or wishes the individual finds…too shameful, too obscene, too dangerous—by attributing them to another." One could see this reversal at work in the staging of Camille Saint-Saen's opera, *Samson et Dalila*, in Antwerp in May 2008, with the Philistines cast in the role of the Israelites and the Israelites as the oppressors of the Philistines.

Certainly, the evidence of mounting anti-Jewish sentiment not only among the intellectual classes but among the European laity as well cannot be doubted. Recent polls and studies reveal a 54% rise in antisemitic incidents in Western Europe, with Holland taking the lead, followed by France, Britain and Belgium. That Israeli officials are subject to impeachment if they land on British soil, or that a Spanish court has been considering, under the principle of "universal jurisdiction," prosecuting Israeli leaders for "war crimes," is only par for the course. As is the fact that not a single major Islamic political figure, responsible for promoting jihad or for committing terrorist provocations, is under legal threat in Spain, the U.K., or any other European country. Terror-sponsoring and genocidal advocate Ahmadinejad, for example, travels freely.

But the form in which antisemitism reveals itself most conspicuously in the current historical moment is the political and media quarantining of the state of Israel, chiefly under the septic influence of the ubiquitous Left.[2] Jew-hatred has been lateralized, so to speak, as ostracism of the Jewish state. The notorious Mohammed al-Durah con is a prime example of the media and official complot against Israel. The Palestinian 12-year old, ostensibly shot by the IDF (Israel Defense Forces) at the Netzarim Junction in Gaza on September 30, 2000—an "event" circulated by the government-controlled-and-financed France TV 2 and picked up by every major news outlet in the world—was almost certainly staged by pro-Palestinian interests.

This phony episode is worth looking at in some detail as it has acquired something like representative status and continues to resonate in the court of public opinion, although the evidence of the hoax is now irrefutable: the fact that only 55 seconds of plainly edited footage was aired for the public; that France 2's chief correspondent Charles Enderlin, who narrated the episode, was not even present at the scene and that the Palestinian cameraman employed by the network, Talal Abu-Rahma, later retracted his testimony (via a fax sent to France 2's Jerusalem offices on September 30, 2002, claiming that his original testimony of October 3, 2000 was given under duress); that the initially hidden film segment showed the boy moving after his "death" and that the photo of the "victim" released to the press was that of a boy older then 12, a certain Rami Jamal al-Durah, admitted to the hospital on the previous day.

There are many other disturbing facts which call the entire story into serious doubt: the two fingers visible in the seventh spliced segment indicating a second take; the party-like atmosphere in the street prior to the skirmish—outtakes from other news agencies, such as AP and Reuters, clearly reveal the rehearsed nature of the scene, including trial ambulance runs; that only seven bullet holes were seen on the wall behind the boy in what was, according to the cameraman, a continuous, 45 minute firefight; that the "dead" child was brought to hospital in late morning although the shooting occurred in mid-afternoon—Arlette Chabot, director of France 2's editorial team, accounted for the discrepancy by presuming "some kind of time change that day in Gaza"; and France 2's refusal to release 27 minutes of original raw footage, among a plethora of such counteracting circumstances. (As of this writing, France 2 has released only 18 minutes of the 27 minute tape. It has apologized, though, for airing old footage, filmed years before the event, incriminating Israel during Operation Cast Lead in Gaza).

Ballistics expert Jean-Claude Schlinger testified before a French court that the bullets that allegedly killed the boy "could not have been the result of Israeli gunfire," corroborating claims that the shocking footage was doctored. And as French philosopher and psychoanalyst Gérard Huber has conclusively shown in his book on the subject,

Contre-expertise d'un mise en scène, the "al-Durah affair" was a prefab piece of theater, planned well in advance and studiously rehearsed, with the intent of further delegitimizing the Jewish state. This is perhaps the most obvious chapter in the never-ending and constantly mutating blood-libel against the Jewish people. It is the Dreyfus affair *redivivus*. That eight years after the original episode the French Court of Appeals overturned a lower court decision against Philippe Karsenty, head of the Media Ratings website, who had been sued for defamation after he challenged the veracity of the France 2 scoop, has not had much effect on demythologizing the scandal.

The mainstream media have been strangely quiet about the second trial and its verdict in Karsenty's favour, giving the news not even a fraction of the coverage it lavished on the original event which it accepted at face value. Burying the calumny plainly has face-saving value, but it also allows the media to shelter its anti-Israeli docket from public scrutiny. Significantly, the media have refused to recognize that the true story, with all its emblematic implications, is not al-Durah, who was either shot by his own people as a "martyr" for the cause or not shot at all but spirited away after the event. The true story is the case of the Egyptian child suffering from cystic fibrosis who could be cured only by a medicine produced in Israel, called Creon 1000, which the Egyptian Ministry of Health has refused to import or accept. The fact that a child who might be *saved* by an Israeli product but is left to malinger and possibly die is the true story of the Muslim Middle East. (See *Al-Ahram*, September 20, 2008.)

This is in the nature of things. Whether it is Mohammed al-Durah, or the clueless Rachel Corrie who was accidentally killed when she placed herself before an Israeli bulldozer blocking an arms-smuggling tunnel and was immediately beatified as a victim of Israeli "brutality," or any of the innumerable fabricated episodes during the Second Lebanon War and Operation Cast Lead in Gaza intended to demonize Israel, all exposed by accurate scrutiny as complete frauds, the topers in the meadhall of the Israel-bashing consensus will not be easily persuaded to end the party. They are having far too good a time of it. For the Jew has once again been gibbeted, in the shape of an Israeli, a Zionist or a member of some immoral "lobby" subtly dominating the public arena—today's detergent version of *The Protocols of the Elders of Zion*.

3

The Shadow Library

There is now a rapidly growing library of anti-Israeli articles, essays and books which abound with the sort of malevolent tropes we have been considering. Indeed, it would require a veritable Bodleian to accommodate them all. Let us examine a representative sample of what is called the "literature" in this chapter.

Who can forget Tony Judt's article in *The Nation* (January 3, 2005), "Goodbye to All That?", in which he asserted that contemporary U.S. foreign policy "is in some respects mortgaged to Israel" and that "to say that Israel and its lobbyists have an excessive and disastrous influence on the policies of the world's superpower is a statement of fact"? The discrepancy between the mannerly "in some respects" and the intemperate "excessive and disastrous" is typical of Judt's writerly stance, in which a raw personal animus breaks through the veneer of scholarly pretence. The initial deference to his subject was always a sham and disqualifies him as a respectable analyst who might be taken seriously. And in any case, President Obama's Middle East policy has clearly put the lie to what was indisputably a gross exaggeration. Then, of course, we have John Mearsheimer's and Stephen Walt's brazen propaganda essay, "The Israel Lobby," which proceeded via the age-old techniques of omission, exaggeration, factual error and selective quotation. This cloacal effort was expanded and published in 2007 as *The Israel Lobby and US Foreign Policy* on, of all mensual dates, September 11. No better was Michael Massing's wretched screed in *The New York Review of Books* (June 8, 2006), stressing Jewish money, listing the names of Jewish neoconservatives, and charring the Jewish Lobby for supporting Israeli territorial expansion.

Another instance of this tendency to besmirch the Jewish state and to call the loyalty of American Jews into question is provided by Max Rodenbeck, the *Economist*'s Middle East correspondent and author of

Cairo: The City Victorious. Rodenbeck published a review/article in the *New York Review of Books* (November 30, 2006) attacking what he regards as the grandiose folly of the American-led "war on terror." Among a long list of indictments, he manages to slip in his anti-Israeli/anti-Jewish bias under cover of chastising America for its sins and misconceptions, glossing over the danger of a nuclear Iran (while not even mentioning its threat to obliterate Israel by nuclear holocaust), contemning Menachem Begin's Irgun guerrillas for "having slaughtered scores of Palestinian citizens and British soldiers" (while skimming right over the thousands of Jews slaughtered in Arab riots and wars and killed or incarcerated by the British), and shriving Islam of its violent propensities, which are rooted in surah after surah of the Koran and in the hadith, as "a product not of Islamic scripture but of the current historical circumstance."

Moreover, one of the reasons, apparently, for American geopolitical behaviour is the "influence of neoconservatives"—although only two "neocon" commentators are named, David Frum and Charles Krauthammer, both Jewish—"and of the pro-Israeli lobby, perceiving a chance to set a superpower on Israel's enemies." Not content with retailing this bit of obloquy, Rodenbeck then goes on to imply that "the Palestinian issue" is one of the "causes of violence" behind the murderous acts of al-Qaeda, utterly disregarding bin Laden's proclaimed intent to restore the Islamic Caliphate to its rightful sphere of dominance.

One of the most prominent instances of this reptilian literature may be found in former president Jimmy Carter's influential book, *Palestine Peace Not Apartheid*, worth examining in some detail. The weave of lies that binds its pages is shocking: UN Resolution 242 demands that Israel return to Palestinians *all* land captured in the 1967 war (false), the West Bank *is* Palestine (false), Israel is an apartheid state as per the title (false), the PLO has never advocated the annihilation of Israel (false), Israel launched a pre-emptive strike against Jordan (false), the security barrier is a "great wall" (false) and is built "entirely within Palestinian territory" (false), no Israeli-Arabs are in the governing cabinet (false), the Israelis "have never granted any appreciable autonomy to the Palestinians" (false), terrorism is only a response to

Israeli actions (false), Hamas has "meticulously observed a cease-fire commitment" (false) and has refrained from terrorist activity since 2004 (false), Saudi Arabia "can be a crucial and beneficial force in the Middle East" (false), Israel is responsible for the exodus of Christians from the Holy Land (false), Israel is guilty for the breakdown of the Camp David peace talks (false), the Israeli Camp David peace plan entailed a "honeycomb of settlements and their interconnecting conduits [that would] entirely divide the West Bank into at least two noncontiguous areas and multiple fragments" (false), "Palestinian leaders unequivocally accepted" the road map (false), there is little discussion about Israeli policies in the United States owing to "powerful political, economic, and religious forces" which ensure that "Israeli government decisions are rarely questioned or condemned" (false), "voices from Jerusalem dominate in our media" (false), among many other consummate mendacities.

Carter, whose world-famous Peace Center is lavishly funded by Saudi Arabia and other Arab donors, has responded in true sybaritic fashion, repeating the old canard that the Israelis are pushing to create a "Greater Israel," an allegation which is patently untrue. The object of his suspicion should rather be the Syrian Social Nationalist Party in Lebanon, which advocates a Greater Syria encompassing Lebanon, Iraq, Jordan, the Palestinian Authority, Israel, Kuwait and Cyprus. But the former US President, who was largely responsible for giving us the Iran we see today—he lauded Ayatollah Khomeini as a "holy man"—and was by all accounts a friend and associate of Yasser Arafat, is not about to modify his position vis à vis Israel. His appearance on Al-Jazeera television, in which he extenuated Palestinian rocket fire aimed at Israel, pointedly refused to pronounce against suicide bombings and claimed that "most of the condemnation of my book came from Jewish-American organizations," was unambiguous. Carter had nothing to say about the fact that fourteen members of his Peace Center's Board of Councilors, including his longtime friend and executive director of the Center, Kenneth Stein, resigned in protest over the book's egregious distortions. (Even the maps provided in the book to chart what Carter sees as Israel's territorial scheming are inaccurate and perhaps intentionally "reconfigured," to use Stein's word. For a set of authentic maps, see Benny Morris' *One State, Two States*.)

Nor did Carter show the slightest repentance in his op-ed piece for the *Washington Post* of January 18, 2007 in which he maligned "most of the vocal American Jewish community" and lent his authority to the factoid that Hamas Prime Minister Ismael Haniyeh "has expressed support for talks between President Mahmoud Abbas and Israeli Prime Minister Ehud Olmert and pledged to end Hamas's rejectionist position if a negotiated agreement is approved by the Palestinian people"—none of which is true. As regards Mahmoud Abbas' franking public school textbooks inciting hatred against Israel and the fact that studies indicate that nearly 80% of Palestinian children aspire to becoming "martyrs", nary a word. Following the Hamas putsch in Gaza, Carter spoke at the Forum on Human Rights held Dublin in June 2007 where he condemned the American refusal to fund Hamas as a "criminal action" and castigated not only the U.S. but, quite preposterously, Israel as well for doing "everything they could to deter a compromise between Hamas and Fatah." Carter adheres to the doctrine of Replacement Theology—replacing the primacy of Israel with that of the Church in God's prophetic timetable—which renders his position partially understandable but does not acquit him of the charges of shoddy scholarship, promotional deception, arrant hypocrisy and thoroughgoing prejudice.[3] Nor should we forget that this *soi-disant* defender of the rights of the dispossessed has not moved to restore his family land to the descendants of the Lower Creek Indians—land from which, as he admits in his book, they were forced "to make room for our white ancestors."

Carter has just produced a follow-up book, *We Can Have Peace In The Holy Land: A Plan That Will Work*. Its gravamen, though perhaps somewhat less offensive, is not appreciably different from that of its predecessor and is not worth wasting paper on. Considering what we already knew and given the remarks he made about Israel's "persecution of the Palestinians" in a panel discussion at his Peace Center on January 3, 2008, when he announced his book's forthcoming publication, we should not have been surprised by the appearance of the same hackneyed fustian. The Saudis will no doubt be pleased to know that Carter honours his commitments and is prepared to work for his money.

The lies and slanders continue to spread like wildfire in the dry season. Harvard professor Patrice Higonnet has tossed another lighted match into the stake-tinder, entitled *Attendant Cruelties*, in which he dutifully attacks the Bush administration, bemoans its neoconservative "sensibility," compares the Jewish conservative philosopher Leo Strauss to the Muslim Brotherhood's leading theorist and propagandist Sayyid Qutb, lacquers Iran's nuclear ambitions as self-defense (as do Walt and Mearsheimer), misdescribes Benjamin Netanyahu as a "Jewish fundamentalist," and deplores the influence of—here we go again—the "pro-Israeli lobby" on the conduct of American foreign policy. Higonnet, who was born in Paris and has written several volumes on the history of France, including *Paris: Capital of the World*, should have been better placed than most to detect the ways in which the anti-Dreyfus libel lends itself to transplantation—most recently, as we have seen, in the al-Durah affair, but also in book after blog after position paper. Certainly his knowledge of American and Israeli history seems copied verbatim out of the Left's ideological playbook.

Of course, self-loathing Jewish anti-Zionists, such as the aforementioned Tony Judt, are among the worst offenders, proliferating like ticks and lice on the body of their people. Their names could fill an almanac of the damned—I list a considerable number of these in a subsequent chapter. A recent case in point, adding to this litany of ignominy, is Max Blumenthal, posting in the *Huffington Post* for July 1, 2009. Blumenthal has the *chutzpah* to claim that Israel is "as brutal as Iran" and that the fate of the young woman Neda Agha-Sultan, murdered in cold blood by Iranian security forces during the recent protests in Tehran, is a common one among the Palestinians. That people actually believe such unbelievable trash is itself almost beyond belief.

Blumenthal may be Jewish but he is just another antisemitic hack, wielding his pen to fill the shelves of the shadow library. Perhaps even more demoralizing is the sight of a *reputable* historical thinker, who also happens to be Jewish, joining the crowd of duplicitous scriveners. One might have thought better of Jacob Heilbrunn who, in *They Knew They Were Right: The Rise of the Neocons*, laments the imputed Jewish influence in determining the direction of the neoconservative movement. Either deleting or playing down the resonant names of its non-Jewish proponents—names like William Bennett, Jeane Kirkpatrick, Michael Novak, Donald Rumsfeld, John Bolton, and Daniel Patrick Moynihan, to mention only a few—he argues that the non-Jewish members of the coterie "were largely bound to the group by a shared commitment to the largest, most important Jewish cause: the survival of Israel." This is utterly tendentious and one could compile a list of such names for whom Israel was, at best, a tertiary preoccupation. Nevertheless, Heilbrunn goes on to assert that neoconservatism is "a Jewish phenomenon, reflecting a subset of Jewish concerns" and that it is "a cultural proclivity specific to American Jews of a certain generation"—there is no mention of the rather telling fact that American Jews vote Democrat over Republican by a ratio of almost 4:1. And we know which of the two parties wavers on Israel and which tends to support it. He then bemoans the pro-Israel state of mind in certain official circles which "must be counted as a neoconservative success," and maintains that it has now become a mediocre "self-perpetuating elite." Heilbrunn's accredited intellectual stature, despite the measured tones and archival spadework that lends authority and lustre to his work, should have precluded so evident a historical bias. The nimbus begins to flicker when even the better minds—*if* that is what they are—enrol in what we might call The Anti-Israel Lobby.

The counsels of the Rodenbecks and Higonnets *et al.* of our political circus have recently surfaced in the lucubrations of Alistair Crooke, formerly a special adviser to EU envoy Javier Solana and founder of the Conflicts Forum, who in the *London Review of Books* (Vol. 29, No. 13) self-assuredly asserts that the hardline approach to Islamism, along with the refusal to countenance the more amenable elements in the Muslim world, is "opening a space, not for moderate pro-Western secularists…but for those who believe that to build a new society you must first burn down the old one." The Arab world, Crooke seems to believe, is obviously crawling with pro-Western secularists just waiting for the opportunity to construct open, liberal democracies, confine the influence of the Koran to the mosque and the private sphere, recognize Israel's right to exist within secure and defensible borders, and neutralize the family compact paradigm that has governed the Muslim world from the beginning of its recorded history. Crooke, like so many others on the "rational Left," is dreaming in jihadicolor.

No longer content to postulate a frivolous separation between "extremists" and "moderates," Crooke and those like him have now come up with a supersubtle distinction between "Islamism" and those "moderate Islamist movements" such as—wait for it—Hamas and the Muslim Brotherhood. Anyone who has troubled to scan the charters of these organizations and follow their actions in a real-world setting would be right to wonder what planet the Crookes and Solanas of the diplomatic Left are living on—a planet on which exotic beings like moderate extremists are part of the natural fauna. But we must have our nursery icons: Santa Claus, the Easter Bunny, the Tooth Fairy, and the moderate extremist. Unless, as it may be, our ideologists know very well what they are doing, that they are something more than merely "useful idiots" (or what columnist Barbara Kay wittily calls "useful jihidiots"). Siding with the enemy, they belong to the fraternity of those whom Mark Lilla, in his book of that title, has dubbed "reckless minds." Lilla has also coined the term "philotyrannical intellectual" which he applies to those who, "consumed with dangerous fantasies," actively choose to ally themselves with the forces of irrationalism and impenitent power. His nomenclature seems fitting.

Be that as it may, a "moderate Islamist movement," the home of the "thoughtful Islamist," is an oxymoron that exists nowhere but in the fevered imagination of the professional negotiator, the political partisan and the ever-compliant media. In a June 25, 2007 release, the BBC informs us that Hamas "espouse[s] a more moderate brand of Islamist politics" than al-Qaeda. This is like saying it's better to be killed with a gun than a bomb. Moreover, the broadcaster lays it down that Hamas has "always shunned al-Qaeda's advances." It is obviously ignorant of the famous poster showing Hamas' spiritual leader Sheikh Ahmed Yassin posing beside Osama bin Laden, of Sheikh Abd al-

Majid al-Zindani, a bin Laden operative, addressing a Hamas fundraiser in March 2006, and of the mounting evidence that the 2003 attack on Mike's Place bar in Tel Aviv, carried out by suicide bombers holding British passports, was a joint al-Qaeda/Hamas operation—the two British-Muslim terrorists were members of the al-Qaeda-linked Islamic *Al Muhajiroun* and were hosted by Hamas in the Gaza Strip.

Logically speaking, what can the term "moderate Islamist" actually mean? Is there such a thing as a "moderate" Nazi, a "moderate" fascist, a "moderate" Bolshevik? If a "moderate" is one who continues to insist on the necessity of destroying Israel, cosseting a nuclear Iran and pursuing the war against the West, what then is an "extremist"?[4] Compare President Barack Obama's intention of "reaching out" to "moderate Taliban"—a moderate Talibanist is one who forbids music, legislates dress, prohibits the education of women, destroys the cultural monuments of other peoples, imposes the most rigid form of shari'a, despises the West and works against its interests, and practices indiscriminate violence in the pursuit of his aims. We should be grateful, I suppose, that the President refuses to treat with extreme Taliban elements.

The diplomatic appeasement of the radical terrorist combines will only allow them to regroup, prepare for further hostilities, strengthen their military hand and extend their reach far into the future, as happened precisely in 1936 when a British-brokered détente permitted the Grand Mufti of Jerusalem to gather his forces and rain even more havoc in the region. But Crooke and his fellow oracles are not to be deflected by swidden reality from their pampered and gratuitous reading of events: the West, and especially the U.S., are responsible for the breakdown of order in Gaza by refusing to treat with Hamas; the unprovoked attack on Israel by Hizbullah in summer 2006 plainly had nothing to do with Iranian strategy but was really a "U.S.-backed war to destroy Hizbullah in Lebanon"; Western policy is alienating and radicalising the as-yet uncommitted Muslim world; and the "domestic Israel lobby" in the U.S. continues to pursue its sinister intent toward abetting Israel's "hegemonic ambitions." The highlight reel hooey of such convictions might be almost entertaining did it not cut the sinews of our preparedness.

Crooke, like many others, welcomes with unseemly warmth the Arab-Palestinian argument for a bi-national state as the only viable solution to the conflict in the Holy Land—in other words, the end of Israel as we know it—and blithely accepts the accusation that Israel has "salami-sliced" the West Bank with its "army posts, military zones, fences and Israeli-only roads"—the familiar anti-checkpoint argument that pretends there is no such creature as a Palestinian suicide bomber on his way to butcher as many Israeli civilians as a thoughtful Islamist can possibly take with him. Whether they are innocents or manipulators, Crooke and his ilk have cause and effect reversed: the checkpoints do not foment terrorism, terrorism created the need for checkpoints, as anyone with a brain in his head can see. No sooner had the checkpoint at the Ariel Junction—the scene of several drive-by shootings and suicide bombings in the past—been lifted than a shooting attack on Israeli civilians followed. Nor did terrorists take long to strike when the checkpoint at the Shuafat crossing in northern Jerusalem was dismantled; 20-year-old Rami Zoari was shot and died of her wounds shortly after.

Crooke's reliance on UN maps and documents—the Monopoly money of today's intellectual currency—to make his case is evidence of either credulity or bad faith. Crooke is also unwilling to admit what both the Israeli and Palestinian administrations know, that it is Israel with its checkpoints, intelligence services and anti-terrorist raids which keeps the weak and beleaguered Fatah regime from toppling as a victim to Hamas insurgency. Nor does he question the fact that some sixty years after the UN partition plan paved the way for the creation of the Jewish state, Israel remains unrepresented on maps and globes in the Arab countries—a Fatah anniversary poster portrays the area where Israel should be as screened by a portrait of Yasser Arafat, a keffiyeh and a rifle. That he quotes favourably Hizbullah terror chieftain Hassan Nasrallah, and refers to Adala as a "human rights organisation based in Israel" without pausing to mention that it is an Arab institution which aims to undo the character of the Jewish state, is *pro forma*. But that he has the temerity to recycle the disreputable Ilan Pappe's spurious and malicious claim that Israel has engaged in a campaign of "ethnic cleansing" clearly reveals where his real sympathies lie.

I go on at some length since Crooke, in himself not a particularly significant figure, is nevertheless an exemplary one. The Crooke agenda, for example, has recently been reinforced by Augustus Richard Norton, a prolific writer on the Middle East, whose new book, *Hezbollah: A Short History*, goes out of its way to launder the Islamic terrorist organization. While providing much useful data on the formation of the Lebanese state, Norton contextualizes Hizbullah as a legitimate expression of the socially deprived Shi'a community "linked to the dispossessed Palestinians, Islamism, and reformism." Norton proceeds to describe Hizbullah's victims as "legitimate resistance targets," dismisses the word "terrorist" as a "rhetorical bludgeon" whose purpose is to "dehumanize radical or revolutionary groups," justifies Hizbullah's attacks on Israel as part of an effort to free prisoners, including those whom he insists "were merely suspects…held hostage," and—if my eyes are not deceiving me—accounts for the rockets falling on Israel as merely anti-aircraft fire which missed their targets. In peddling his pet thesis about the "Lebanonization" of Hizbullah, he makes no mention of the bankruptcy of the terrorist culture represented by Hizbullah and its affiliates—Iran, Syria, and their Palestinian clients—nor of the real situation in which Israel finds itself.

How he might countenance the civil unrest, amounting to a mini-civil war, unleashed by Hizbullah in the streets of Beirut and in other parts of the country in May 2008, or parry the observation of Lebanese political analyst Antoine Basbous (*Liberation* 9, 2008) that Lebanon has been earmarked by Iran as the "scene of operations, a land of Jihad [where] imperialism and Zionism need to be defeated," must remain in the realm of the ineffable. Norton would also have to embark on some difficult maneuvering to explain Hizbullah's violation of the 1989 Taif agreement, which provided for the disarmament of the various competing militias. For although Hizbullah was renamed as a "resistance force" against an external foe in order to evade the terms of the proscription, its armed involvement in an *internal* conflict has put it in clear breach of the entente. "Even the Israeli enemy didn't dare do in Beirut what Hizbullah has done," said Lebanese Prime Minister Fuad Saniora. But Norton would surely find a way to exonerate his favourite terror group. And Israel would doubtlessly figure as scapegoat. All of which makes me think of the old light bulb joke formula, a variant of which might be apt in the circumstances. How many Islamists does it take to change a light bulb? None. We do it for them.

To speak now of my own country: This sort of claptrap, somewhat diluted, is featured in Canada's self-proclaimed newspaper of record, *The Globe and Mail*, whose chief columnist Jeffrey Simpson accuses Prime Minister Stephen Harper's Conservative government of "align[ing] the country with the preferences of the Canada-Israel Committee" (January 16, 2007). According to this most orgulous of pundits, it is an approach that "helps one country in the region, and hurts everywhere else." Simpson would have Canadian foreign policy revert to its so-called "honest broker" standing, which in the past, under the Liberal administration favoured by Simpson, meant voting with almost every pro-Palestinian and anti-Israeli resolution passed by the United Nations. This is not the first time that Simpson has referred to the nefarious influence of the Canada-Israel Committee, which in his Bothers Grimm world, inhabited by godmother Liberals and wicked Conservatives, has acquired the stamp of a Canadian Jewish lobby—as if the Jewish community has not regularly voted *en bloc* for the Liberal party and as if the far more veridical Muslim lobby, consisting of such groups as the Canadian Islamic Congress, the Islamic Society of North America Canada and the Canadian Council on American-Islamic Relations, were not shriller, more insistent, more thin-skinned and, from the outlook of growing electoral clout, considerably more effective.

Such apologists, to borrow the title of Aaron Klein's recent book, are only *Schmoozing with Terrorists*—and not to gather information, as did Klein, but in mindless sympathy with their aims. But it goes further than merely schmoozing. The hate-merchants are in effect "travelling" with the terrorists and doing a very brisk business in the process when it comes to Israel. The trouble, too, is that these varioloid attitudes are not confined only to the "intellectual elite" but filter down into popular culture as well, as we saw on the *Law and Order: Criminal Intent* television series. Its February 27, 2007 installment featured a Jewish police captain colluding with Israeli intelligence to compromise an investigation, Israeli bulldozers levelling Palestinian schools and a character alluding to "Israeli brutality." NBC subsequently issued a statement claiming that "the program is fictional and does not depict any actual person or event." But anti-Israel stereotypes have always been fictional, which has not prevented them from feeding into the collective hatefest against Jews and the marathon of disinformation against the Jewish state.

Another such salient example comes from best-selling detective novelist Steve Berry who, in developing a character for his *The Alexandria Link*, which begins in 1948, takes it as given that: "Just yesterday the Jewish underground had attacked a nearby village. Forty Palestinian men and women were herded into a quarry and shot. *Nothing unusual.* Arabs were being systematically murdered and expelled. Land that their families had occupied for sixteen hundred years was being confiscated" (emphasis added). There is no sense that the author is employing the technique of "free indirect speech," expressive of his character's own thought processes. The *Library Journal* was unintentionally accurate when it puffed the book as follows: "Contemporary issues and page-turning thriller elements combine with history in shocking ways." When such selective exaggerations and one-sided historical abridgments as I have excerpted here are understood as part of a character's beliefs, as part of the *fiction*, the technique is perfectly acceptable—as in G.E. Lessing's acclaimed play, *The Jews*, where antisemitic views are held by a particular character, who is later cured of his prejudices. But when such distortions are presented as an objective fact on which to ground a character's motives, then we have either straight propaganda or unforgivable ignorance.

Paul McGeough's *Kill Khalid: The Failed Assassination of Khalid Mishal and the Rise of Hamas*, which has just come out, is another such corrupt and misleading tract, idealizing one of the bloodiest of terrorist masterminds. Among its many, probably deliberate howlers, McGeough claims that the Zionists "demanded all of historical Palestine" when the documented truth is that they accepted partition, as witness the 1937 Peel Commission and the 1947 United Nations Partition Plan, which mapped out two independent states. Both proposals were assented to by the Zionists and rejected by the Arabs. McGeough goes on to paint a roseate picture of Palestinian farmers which properly belongs in a fairy tale, cannot refrain from sniping at the Jewish Lobby, and focuses on Israeli "brutality" while glorifying Palestinian "resistance." That McGeough earns his living as a journalist is *pro forma.*

In the miasma of popular sentiment, fiction and truth can scarcely be distinguished. From the standpoint of anti-Jewish sentiment in particular, fiction and truth are epistemological isomorphs and cannot be separated from one another. Which is to say, fiction becomes truth and truth, fiction. Unfortunately, the malediction of Isaiah has been forgotten or dismissed: "Woe unto them that call evil good, and good evil; that put darkness for light, and light for darkness…"

But there may be a certain ironic justice inexorably at work in the Devil's athenaeum I have described. This inversion has now become standard procedure. Israel and its people, whom Isaiah called "a light unto the nations," are now threatened by an encroaching darkness. But so, as it turns out, are we all. If I did not believe in the preservation of books regardless of their content, I would say that this is one library that merits burning since none of us are exempt from its evil influence. We know the old saw about the canary in the coal mine, which we should do well to keep in mind. It has rarely been more appropriate than now. For the shadow library ultimately casts its stygian murk over Jews and non-Jews alike.

4

The Roadblock to Peace

The affective response to Israel across the world has been luted with a mixture of ideological prejudice and reflex hostility, which serves to keep it mindproof. Such unreasoning hatred explains why, in the interminable conflict raging in the Middle East, the Palestinians have been given carte blanche. Every atrocity they commit is whitewashed as "resistance" while the Israelis are slagged for "state terrorism" and every act of Israeli self-defense is blazoned as a "disproportionate response" if not as a "massacre." What would qualify as "proportionate force" in cases where the attackers routinely and deliberately operate from within civilian areas is a question that is conveniently avoided. It is why any Israeli response to Gaza rocket fire is condemned as "collective punishment" and a violation of international norms by the United Nations, which has no problem turning a blind eye on the continuing barrage of Kassams fired from Gaza at the homes, businesses, schools and kindergartens of Sderot. It is why the press has bowdlerized the word "terrorist" and substituted inoffensive synonyms like "militant," "activist" and "insurgent." It is why in news media like the BBC, as Andrei S. Markovits points out in *Uncouth Nation: Why Europe Dislikes America*, Palestinian "acts of violence are described using the passive voice or in an impersonal manner, such as 'a bomb was placed'..." whereas "Israelis, by contrast, are portrayed as operative actors: They 'murder,' 'kill,' 'destroy,' and 'attack'—and are also given adjectives like 'brutal,' 'gruesome,' and 'merciless.' "

The latest scandals involving the BBC are the revelation that one of its employees is a member of Hamas, which is officially proscribed as a terrorist organization in Britain; the posting of a blatantly antisemitic message on its Radio Web site, signed by one "Iron Naz," which it refused to remove; its referring to the assassinated arch-terrorist Imad Mughniyeh as a "great national leader"; and on July 2, 2008, when a

Palestinian terrorist rammed a giant Caterpillar along a busy Jerusalem street, killing three people and injuring more than sixty, the BBC's initial headline read: "Israel bulldozer driver shot dead." The BBC later referred to the Jewish Center attacked by the Mumbai terrorists as an "office building." The BBC's Middle East editor Jeremy Bowen has been overtly and consistently biased against Israel in his media articles and reports, accusing Israeli officers of having "unfinished business" going back to the War of Independence, maintaining without the slightest documentation that the U.S. regarded the Har Homa settlement as illegal, and claiming that Israel was in defiance of international law—this without any citation of the relevant articles, which would have proven otherwise. And naturally, where even a modicum of sympathy or understanding of the Israeli position is trotted out, it is almost immediately hyphenated by the flummery of moral equivalence, as if there were some sort of parity between self-defense and murderous aggression.

This knee-jerk reaction to Israel explains why Gaza was allowed to Hizbullize itself while the world looked the other way. It accounts for the fact that Human Rights outfits and NGOs have been hijacked by the anti-Israeli crowd hiding behind their prophylactic titles. It is the reason, as Ruth Wisse wrote in *Jews and Power*, that the Palestinians "have become the only nationalism to be recognized by the United Nations *prior* to statehood." Indeed, the Palestinians are the only (self-described) irredentist group in the world with their own UN committee—the pompous-sounding Committee on the Exercise of the Inalienable Rights of the Palestinian People—as well as UN observer status, a privilege no other stateless group, neither Tibetans, Kurds, Tamils or Basques, currently enjoys. It is the reason that the rejection by the 1974 Palestinian National Council of UN Resolution 242 because it recognized Israeli sovereignty is never mentioned. (The PLO's 1988 acceptance of 242 is often showcased as a sign of Palestinian good faith, but the fact that this "acceptance" was essentially nullified by the retention in the Palestinian National Covenant of the articles calling for the destruction of Israel and the expulsion of the Jews is kept tightly under wraps. The fine words of Yasser Arafat recognizing various UN Resolutions and renouncing terrorism were equally hollow, as the sequel proved beyond the slightest doubt.) It throws light upon the general refusal to acknowledge that the *casus belli* in the region is not a wrangle over borders but the Palestinian rejection of both the concept and reality of a *Jewish state*, which is why the *Haq al-Awda* or "right of return" of millions of foreign-born, manufactured "refugees" has been a non-negotiable issue for the Palestinians, from Arafat to Abbas.

The claim bruited by Arab propagandists, Israeli revisionist historians and the anti-Israeli contingent of academics, political commentators and public intellectuals today that the Palestinian refugees were driven out by Israeli forces during the War of Independence is more than likely only partially, and perhaps minimally, valid. Even Sir John Glubb of "Glubb Pasha" fame, the British general of the Arab Legion conducting a campaign of "ethnic cleansing" against the newborn Jewish state, wrote in the *London Daily Mail* for August 12, 1948 that "The Arab civilians panicked and fled ignominiously. Villages were frequently abandoned before they were threatened by the progress of war." Many Arab public figures and news sources of the time were equally scathing; for example, Emile Ghoury, secretary of the Palestinian Arab Higher Committee, interviewed in the *Beirut Telegraph* for September 6, 1948, stressed that "these refugees [are] the direct consequence of the act of the Arab states in opposing partition and the Jewish state," the Near East Arabic Broadcasting Station in Cyprus reminded its listeners on April 3, 1949 that "the Arab Higher Committee encouraged the refugees' flight from their homes," the Jordanian daily *Falastin* in an article for February 19, 1949 blamed the "Arab states which had encouraged the Palestine Arabs to leave their homes," and the Syrian prime minister at the time, Khaled el-Azm, confessed in his 1973 *Mudhakkirat* (Memoirs) that "it is we who made them leave," among a surfeit of such affidavits.

Thus, when American-Palestinian poet Naomi Shihab Nye memorializes

My father, the fathers and mothers
who lifted no weapon, bending solemnly to tasks
despite trembling lip and hand...

she writes not only in ignorance of the facts, but conveniently forgets the pogroms, riots, slaughter frenzies and military operations that the surrounding Arab nations and the Palestinian Arabs inflicted on thousands of Jews who also "lifted no weapon, bending solemnly to tasks/despite trembling lip and hand." Meanwhile, as the Palestinians assert their right to homestead in Israel, it is taken for granted that no Israelis or Jews will be allowed to settle in Palestine, even in villages where a Jewish presence is ancestral and on land that was mandated by the League of Nations as part of the Jewish nation.

This same anti-Zionist (and anti-Jewish) reflex is the rationale behind the United Nations' perpetual denunciation of Israel, evidenced by the disgraceful example of (now former) UN Human Rights High Commissioner Louise Arbour initially signing onto the Arab "Rights" charter equating Zionism with racism and taking cover afterward under a tympani of UN doublespeak; and by the convening of its preparatory committee for the 2009 UN World Conference Against Racism, or Durban II, which resulted in another travesty of the original ideals of the world body: Libya was chair, Iran was vice-chair, Cuba was rapporteur, and Pakistan, South Africa, Russia, Belgium, Norway and Greece sat on the planning bureau. As the business maxim has it, personnel is policy. It illustrates why all the principals have forgotten or suppressed the unpalatable truth that Jews were expelled from their ancient communities and many slaughtered in the terror campaign initiated by Azzam Pasha, the Arab League Secretary-General at the time of the 1947-48 war. It tells us why there was never the slightest effort, neither from the Arabs nor the international community, to pitch for an independent Palestinian state when the Gaza Strip and the West Bank were part of Egypt and Jordan—or any acknowledgment of the fact that Israel's *bona fide* attempts to negotiate the return of these districts after the 1967 war were met by the three No's of the Khartoum Conference: "No peace, No negotiation, No recognition."

It is the reason that the negotiating Quartet and many Western nations have embraced Fatah chief Mahmoud Abbas with open arms, indifferent to the facts that he is not a "moderate" but a devious incompetent who adheres to the traditional goals of Fatah, and that one of the most powerful figures in the party is Farouk Kaddoumi, a diehard rejectionist and supporter of the politics of terror. (In this sense, Fatah's position is ultimately in accord with that of Hamas: Mahmoud Zahar, former PA foreign minister and a top Hamas official, has declared that recognition of Israel violates the Koran and that the principle of Muslim hegemony over all of Palestine is sacred.) It explains why the Lebanese army was given a free pass in its indiscriminate shelling of the Nahr al-Barad refugee camp where the terrorist group Fatah al-Islam had dug in, causing hundreds of civilian casualties, while every act of Israeli self-defense against a terrorist enemy, which seeks to avoid harming non-combatants, is bannered as an atrocity. It is the reason the loaded term "occupation" is used as a weapon against Israel when the bald facts are that Gaza is an autarchical quasi-state, the West Bank presently controls 94% of its territory, the Palestinian Authority has rejected an Israeli proposal to compensate it by ceding 6% of Israeli land, and in the Palestinian lexicon the term "occupation" refers *to the whole of Israel*. What we do not want to see is that the Israeli state of mind, once the country's defensive needs are served, is largely concessionary, whereas the Palestinian mentality is largely rejectionist.

The anti-Zionist reflex reveals why the "Holocaust effect" has largely evaporated and, in some quarters, has even been turned against Israel and the Jews. It explains why the Palestinian is now regarded as the Holocaust Jew and the Israeli is excoriated as the new Nazi. As Pascal Bruckner argues in *The Temptation of Innocence*, Jews are now considered "unworthy of the role" of being Jewish; the Genocide has been confiscated by other groups in order to acquire "a kind of perpetual line of credit for immortality." And in *La tyrannie de la pénitence*, he carries the idea into the political domain: "*Nazifier les Israéliens, c'est délégitimer l'Etat…c'est aussi judaiser les Arabes…C'est enfin justifier à l'avance l'eventuelle disparition d'Israël…*" ("Nazifying the Israelis is delegitimizing the State…it is also Judaizing the Arabs…It is finally to justify in advance the eventual disappearance of Israel.") It is why Israel is frequently compared to "illegitimate" colonial sediments like the Boers in South Africa, the British settlers in the former Rhodesia or the French *pieds noirs* in Algeria—when the historical reality is that the link to the

Jewish past in the Holy Land is unbroken and that this link has in many places been ingeminated by legal purchase as well. Israel's great crime is simply to be. And it explains why the hoary tactics of *Schrecklichkeit* have been pardoned in much of the West as a diplomatic supplement in the Palestinian repository of ways and means.

It makes no difference that Israel was the only country to recognize the Arab State of Palestine in 1948, which was in any case immediately swallowed up by the surrounding Arab belligerent nations. It makes no difference that Israel supplies Gaza with most of its water and electricity, which is to say, at the cost of the Israeli taxpayer. It makes no difference that Israeli-Arabs possess the franchise and are represented by elected members in the Knesset and the governing Cabinet, whereas Jews do not enjoy a comparable privilege in any Muslim country, with the sole exception of Bahrain, the most "progressive" of the region's Arab states, where Huda Azar Nunu, a descendant of the tiny Jewish community dating back to Talmudic times, sits on the legislative body. (Yet, as of this writing, Bahrain is moving toward re-opening its Israel Boycott Office and its legislature has recommended ending all formal contacts with the "Zionist entity.") Nor is the fact ever mentioned that the first Arab women to exercise the vote were those who live in Israel. It makes no difference that an independent "Palestine" adjacent to Israel would be officially *Judenrein*, or Jew-free, which means it would not be a democratic state. It makes no difference that the Palestinian Arabs have failed or reneged *in every area* of their commitments to Israel and the "peace process," from putting the lid on media incitement to debelling the terrorists in their ranks to reforming the school curriculum—indeed, Palestinian education is reminiscent of that passage in Orwell's *Animal Farm* in which the dominant pigs train puppies to become attack dogs.

It makes no difference that Adolf Hitler is openly celebrated on Palestinian radio while the Holocaust has been edited out of Palestinian schoolbooks. It makes no difference that the Gaza authorities have mounted an exhibit portraying Palestinian children being burned to death in Birkenau-type ovens, a degree of perversity which is almost beyond conceiving. It makes no difference that the Palestinians have made a fine art of unaccountability, holding the West hostage to their faux-narrative of historical innocence and wearing down the Israelis by insistently transferring responsibility for political failure and trading on the Israeli desire for peace to create the conditions for an eventual Palestinian victory. And it makes no difference that the Palestinians give every sign of believing that the international community owes them privileged status, that Europe and America owe them perpetual largesse and that Israel owes them its own demolition, but that they owe the world nothing. They have never troubled to build a productive economy but over the years have budgeted chiefly for administrative salaries, propaganda activities, massive supplies of weapons and the maintenance of terrorist militias, not to mention that vast sums that have been siphoned into private accounts.

Indeed, the World Bank accused the Palestinian Authority of hiking its payroll while its GDP continues to fall—despite financial difficulties, it hired 1,300 more civil servants and inducted another 6,800 people into its security forces. According to a survey conducted in the *Jerusalem Report* (December 24, 2007), the PA payroll was in excess of its total revenues. At the same time, more external financial aid had poured into Palestinian coffers in 2006—1.2 billion dollars, an increase of 200 million dollars, is a modest estimate—than in the previous year despite the sanctions imposed on the Hamas regime. A significant proportion of donor aid was transferred to a new PLO account, circumventing the international embargo against the Hamas government. The UN Office for the Coordination of Humanitarian Affairs (OCHA) reports that foreign donations rose by 300% in 2006, and that much of this assistance was channelled through another account called the Temporary International Mechanism (recently relaunched as the PEGASE mechanism with an emphasis on sustainable development projects). Averaged out, the Palestinian subsidy, prior to the Paris Conference of December 17, 2007 which greatly increased the subsidies, exceeded $300 per person; the closest beneficiary-rate at the time pertained to certain African states, at approximately $40 per person.

To inquire where most of this donor infusion has gone betokens an unflappable naivety. The answer is staring us in the face: the reign of the jackboot and the jackpot. With respect to Palestinian Authority, the plain fact is that the ratio between the extent of financial aid and the degree of economic improvement is an inverse one: the more aid that washes in, the more the economic situation deteriorates. As Efraim Inbar, professor in Political Studies at Bar Ilan University and Director of the Begin-Sadat Center for Strategic Studies, points out, "economic aid is only as good as the ability of the recipient's economy and government to use it productively. Therefore, it is doubtful that sending more money to the dysfunctional Palestinian economy will do any good" (*Jerusalem Post*, November 24, 2007).

But this counsel of prudence has had no effect on the behaviour of Western politicians who, at the Paris Conference convened to strengthen Mahmoud Abbas, pumped an additional 7.4 billion dollars into the Palestinian Authority. In 2008, the Americans chipped in another 600 million dollars. The Europeans, like the Americans, are clearly undeterred by the likelihood, amounting to a near certainty, that most of this largesse will disappear into offshore accounts, weapons purchases and yet more security personnel. In fact, at the July 2008 Arab Summit in Damascus, Abbas revealed that the PA pays the salaries of 77,000 Hamas employees in Gaza; the PA also declared its intention to transfer 40% of the European monetary pledge to Hamas! Daniel Pipes calculates that this new windfall translates into $1,400 per West Bank Palestinian per year, the annual salary of the average Egyptian—though we might add that few individual Palestinians will get to spend this money, apart from Yasser Arafat's widow, Suha, who receives an annuity of 22 million dollars to support her Paris lifestyle. Pipes also refers to various reliable studies showing that increased financial aid to such volatile regions correlates robustly with increased terrorist activity (*National Post*, December 18, 2007). In this regard, as they bring off one of the greatest shakedowns in history, the Palestinians certainly give a lot of bang for the buck.

Michael Eisenstadt, director of the Military and Security Studies Program at the Washington Institute, agrees that this latest binge of financial aid will have little or no positive effect. In his Policy Focus

Paper #78 for the Institute, *The Palestinians: Between State Failure and Civil War* (December 2007), he writes that "Although the PA, since its creation in 1994, has functioned as a *de facto* state with a parliament, executive, judiciary, governmental bureaucracy, and security forces, it has…increasingly exhibited many of the pathologies typically associated with the phenomenon of state failure," being unable "to fulfill the most important functions of a state: to provide for the welfare and security of its people. The clearest signs of the weakness of the PA were what Palestinians refer to as 'the four F's': *fawda* (chaos), *fitna* (strife), *falatan* (lawlessness) and *fassad* (corruption)." None of this will end, Eisenstadt cautions, until far-reaching political reforms are achieved, including "the inculcation of a culture of political compromise, and strong leadership—conditions not likely to be fulfilled soon." More money in the absence of structural change will only exacerbate the problem. Indeed, seven months after the Paris Conference, Abbas was busy complaining that the Palestinian Authority was running short of donor money. The PA leader cited tardiness on the part of the grantors. *WorldTribune.com* for August 1, 2008 tells another story: Palestinian "dissidents" have charged that senior PA officials have embezzled millions of dollars of security assistance "to purchase private homes, automobiles and furniture" and "to speculate on the food and fuel markets in the West Bank."

But never mind. In response to Abbas' *cri du coeur*, the European Union announced in August 2008 that it has sent an additional 59 million dollars to the Palestinian Authority, in part to contribute to the maintenance of a power plant in Gaza, as well as funding a 54 million dollar project to upgrade infrastructure. The financial bleeding, as we have seen, continues to this day. After the latest round of Israel/Hamas fighting, the international community has pledged close to $5 billion toward the reconstruction of Gaza, with $900 million coming from the United States. The chances that Hamas will find a way to get its hands on this money and use it for military purposes is a near certainty. In the summer of 2009, the United States, Germany and Japan pledged another $400 million for West Bank infrastructure improvements in water treatment for irrigation purposes and road upgrades. The latest fiscal hemorrhage was announced on July 14, 2009 by the World Bank: another $33.5 million for Palestinian infrastructure initiatives.

All this will certainly make life easier for farmers, drivers and civilians in general. It will also be of great benefit to the terrorist militias.

How is it possible that our political leaders cannot be aware of what is so glaringly obvious? Owing in part to the adoption of the Palestinians as the Noble Savage *du jour* and the foster children of Western bad conscience, in part to the construction of a fiction to appease Western electorates, the underlying truth is that the Palestinians have been sanctified at the expense of the Jews and this is their warrant for existence. What the Palestinians have going for them is the latent—and more often manifest—hatred of Israel and the Zionist enterprise in much of the world, which is only the contemporary permutation of age-old antisemitism and which they can tap into and exploit to their own advantage. This is why the Palestinian narrative has "taken." As Bruckner suspects, the Western embrace of the Palestinians may be nothing more than the furtive policy and privy intention of an international community that wishes for nothing more than to turn Israel into a larnax for the Jewish people. Aside from this, in an intellectually macerated world, there is little willingness to recognize that when terrorism becomes a way of life as it has for the Palestinians, there is scant prospect for peace, "dialogue" becomes only another weapon in the terrorist arsenal and international aid turns into an ATM for the terrorist cause and the enrichment of corrupt potentates.

The dysplasia of Palestinian social and political life is almost never understood as a function of its own inner evolution—or want of such—as evidenced by the rejection of every peace proposal from the time of the British Mandate to the present and by the ongoing partisan violence in Gaza and the West Bank which has turned the road map for peace into a dead letter. For that matter, the road map has never been anything more than a chimerical document projecting a political hallucination. In the years since Oslo, the Palestinians have refused to budge from their "negotiating" position, except in the sense that they have requited every Israeli offer and compromise with a renewed bout of terror. Indeed, the death toll among Israeli civilians was higher in the Oslo peace aftermath than in the entire forty five years of Israel's existence prior to the "peace accord." During the post-Oslo period, the

Israeli public has been educated to accept major concessions to the Palestinians, including "disengagement" from the Territories; during the same period, the Palestinians have been indoctrinated to make no real concessions whatsoever, insisting on the inadmissible principle of the "right of return" which would lead to the demographic end of the Jewish state, and relying on violence rather than arbitration to achieve their ends. What Jonathan Spyer has said about the Syrians in their negotiations with Israel is true also of the Palestinians: they are keen to accept the dowry, but not to embrace the bride.

Reputable specialists on the Middle East familiar with Arabic, such as Norman Spector, former Canadian ambassador to Israel, and Bernard Lewis, among the greatest living authorities on the subject, have observed that the Palestinian message expressed in the original tongue is very different from its "moderate" English doppelgänger: the latter holds out a prospect for peace (though hedged with the usual unconditional demands), the former promises the end of Israel. This is as true of Mahmoud Abbas as it was of Yasser Arafat. Indeed, following the famous handshake on the White House lawn ratifying the Oslo agreement in September 1993, Arafat spoke on Jordanian television assuring his people that Oslo meant the eventual end of Israel, on the model of the ten-year Treaty of Hudabiyah in 628 which was violated by Muhammad two years later. One should keep in mind that the Palestinian objective is conquest, as in the oft-repeated slogan, *min al-nahr ila al-bahr* (from the river to the sea), a claim reinforced by the PA appointed Mufti of Jerusalem, Sheikh Ikrima Sabri, who, speaking on Palestinian TV in January of 2001, told his audience: "From a religious point of view, Palestine from the sea to the river is Islamic." Later in the same year he declared that "the negation of Jewish existence is an existential need of Islam." These sentiments are very much in line with the results of a survey commissioned by the Anwar Sadat Chair for Peace at the University of Maryland which found that the most popular leader in the Arab world is Hizbullah chief Hassan Nasrallah, followed by Syria's Bashar Assad and Iran's Mahmoud Ahmadinejad, all of whom have called for the disappearance of Israel.

Whatever Palestinian ambitions may be, nation-building appears beyond their means. Former American ambassador to Israel Martin S. Indyk argues in *Foreign Affairs* for May 2003 that the "road map" illusion, namely that the Palestinians are ready for statehood, must be replaced by the political concept of trusteeship if a sovereign and self-sustaining Palestine is ever to see the light of history. Six years later the analysis remains intact. Political Journalist Khaled Abu Toameh quotes a Palestinian Authority official who, briefing U.S. special Middle East Envoy George Mitchell, confessed that: "Even if Binyamin Netanyahu were to offer us a Palestinian state tomorrow morning, I'm not sure that we are prepared to meet such a huge challenge" (*The Jerusalem Post*, April 23, 2009).

Failing a new and enlightened Mandate for the West Bank and Gaza, enforced by the Western powers (forget the U.N.), it is highly unlikely that the Palestinians would be able to successfully manage their own independence. And even then, the project would remain doubtful. For the concerted effort at Rolfing the Palestinians toward statehood would generate little more than chronic disharmony or the mere perpetuation of the current anarchy: the patient is simply not ready and there is no forcing the process. The Palestinians have been so dependent on international handouts for the last 60 years that they have absolutely no idea of how to go about forming a state. Indeed, in the face of increasing Palestinian ineptitude, corruption and violence, Indyk has since revised his position to include an international, armed, intercessory force to save the Palestinians from themselves.

In consequence, the "road map" is, in reality, a roadblock, and the various "summits" along the way are only washouts in disguise. I often think that the participants in Middle East peace conferences tend to fall in love with their own metaphors, which they proceed to reify—locutions like "road map," "fast track," "shelf agreement," "time horizon," "window of opportunity," "end game"—and which sound both authoritative and colloquial, generating unreflective assent. Nevertheless, the fact remains that the return of territory—which amounts, let us remember, to around 6% of the West Bank—as a prelude to the Arab recognition of Israel does not seem like a promising strategic move.

As former Israeli Prime Minister Yitzhak Shamir pointed out at the Madrid peace talks in 1991, "There was no hint of recognition of Israel before the war in 1967, when the territories in question were not under Israeli control." (They were under Egyptian and Jordanian control.) Irrespective of whatever spin is put on it for the benefit of public relations or the sunny rodomontade of press releases, the much-touted Annapolis conference was no exception to the general rule of miscarriage and desuetude, though not without causing additional damage, mostly to Israel. Israeli Prime Minister at the time, Ehud Olmert, the weakest and most unqualified in the history of the country and author of that revelatory phrase, "We are tired of winning," did everything in his power to lose. Luckily his attempt to give away the store, as was the case with Ehud Barak at Camp David, was foiled by his putative beneficiaries who wanted the whole block.

Meanwhile, reports have surfaced that the Palestinian negotiating team, representing a rump Palestinian Authority, was riven by internecine squabbles, particularly between former Prime Minister Ahmed Qurei and Geneva Initiative participant, Yasser Abed Rabbo, thereby weakening its ability to deliver on its promises. One such promise was that Israel, should it comply with their demands, would live in "a sea of peace"—might this be the same sea into which Israelis are to be driven? Yet as recent events have demonstrated, the Palestinians cannot even keep order in their own storm-tossed houseboat.

Fresh divisions emerged in May 2009 when Abbas moved to form a new government without consulting his Fatah party and excluding representatives from a powerful internal faction. This rupture further weakens Fatah's ability to negotiate responsibly and partly explains why Abbas, on the day before his May 28 meeting with President Obama, announced his refusal to treat with Israeli Prime Minister Benjamin Netanyahu. With his authority compromised, the only face-saving maneuver open to him was to put the onus for the stalled peace process on his Israeli counterpart. (Following that meeting, Abbas decided to wait for American pressure on Israel to produce dividends for the Palestinians.)

Further, when one considers the *fundamental* Arab/Palestinian demands, like shrinking Israel's borders so that they are rendered indefensible and inundating the country with millions of bogus "refugees," the auguries for eventual reconciliation are nugatory. From the Israeli perspective, the process seems more like committing national suicide than reaching a *modus vivendi*. There is no reason to expect a different result under any future Annapolis II, III or IV, which like Hollywood movie sequels merely grow progressively embarrassing as one clunker wearily follows another. P. David Hornik is on the mark when he suggests that the U.S. administration should adopt "the Israeli understanding of the Middle East as an arena of survival rather than conciliation" (*FrontPageMagazine*, July 6, 2009). Nor does it help that the Palestinians remain trapped in the oddly sustainable rubble of a failed ideology.

Which is Palestine? Gaza or the West Bank, two entities themselves ridden by internal dissension and threatening further mitosis? And when one reflects that Palestinian society has been educated from grassroots to tree tops to hate Israelis, embrace "martyrdom" for the cause and regard peace agreements and international accords as merely another form of ordnance, it should become obvious that we are embarking on the wrong track.

Abbas himself has made this amply clear. Speaking at a memorial rally in Ramallah in October 2008, he pledged that "The Palestinian leadership will continue to follow Yasser Arafat's path until a Palestinian state with Jerusalem as its capital is established.... The path of the shahids—Arafat, George Habash and Sheikh Ahmed Yassin—is the path that we cherish...." Having extolled the three arch-terrorists, his subsequent statements revealed that the Palestinian administration has no interest in flexible and reasoned negotiation: "We rejected Israeli proposals that stipulated making concessions including on Jerusalem and the refugees.... We either get all six points—Jerusalem, settlements, borders, refugees, water and security—or nothing at all." Everything or nothing is as good a description as any of Palestinian negotiating technique and "nothing at all" the most likely result.

The superficial counsels for the success of the Annapolis conference and similar peace initiatives proffered by political throwbacks Zbigniew Brzezinski, Lee Hamilton, Brent Scowcroft and others, which take the Palestinians at their word, ignore Israeli security interests, acknowledge rogue actors like Syria and Hamas, cancel the reasons for Israel's very founding and misconstrue the animating impulse of Arab diplomacy are a surefire recipe for ever greater chaos and hostility in the region (see *The New York Times*, November 8, 2007). Even with the change in the U.S. administration, the Annapolis principles are being held in what housewives call a "cold oven," that is, quietly kept warm until the time comes to serve them up again or raise the temperature.

President Obama's May 28, 2009 meeting with Abbas was only another of these *rechauffés*. PA spokesman Nabil Abu Rudeina had proleptically labelled this encounter "a turning point for the Middle East peace process" (*The Jordan Times*, April 23, 2009). There have, of course, been so many such turning points that one is reminded of the frenzied and hilarious roundabout car chase scene in Peter Sellers' *The Pink Panther*, leading to nothing more than vertigo and the inevitable collision. It is hard to deny the element of bathos and even of farce in these proceedings. Despite visionary hopes and occasional tenebrous indications of some sort of resolution, the "peace process" is going in circles and is kept alive only by a veteran attachment to retro diplomacy—one thinks of Irving Kristol's insightful remark that "Whom the gods would destroy they first tempt to resolve the Arab-Israeli conflict."

Indeed, the Middle East situation is so complex that no diplomatic Bluetooth protocol has yet been invented to facilitate transmission between the many local actors, between the various state powers with interests in the region, and between the local actors and the state powers, all with competing agendas that resist synchronization. An armed standoff, built upon the concept of effective deterrence, is probably the best we can hope for regardless of our underlying desires and assumptions. As Meir Weinstein, director of the Jewish Defense League in Canada has said, pointing out that every peace plan thus far has produced not peace but blood, "We don't believe there's a peace plan out there that's viable…the best you can do is have a security plan."

Weinstein's evaluation is bolstered by the statements of Massad Yousef, the son of popular Hamas leader Sheikh Hassan Yousef, who fled Ramallah and is now living in exile in California. In an interview with *Haaretz.com* (July 31, 2008), he asserts without the slightest hesitation that Israel "will never, but never have peace with Hamas. Islam, as the ideology that guides them, will not allow them to achieve a peace agreement with the Jews…More than that. An entire society sanctifies death and the suicide terrorists."

To believe otherwise, I'm afraid, is to yield to the Sirens who tempt us with our own febrile infatuations, to which Western (and much Israeli) political thought seems incurably predisposed. As Kristol suggested, politicians who embroil themselves in this particular morass must have a masochistic desire to destroy their careers or reputations. To use a chemical metaphor, they have not realized that the "peace process" is essentially a lyophilic process: a dispersed phase (of violence) with a high affinity for a continuous phase (of violence).

An addled President Bush and his presbyopic Secretary of State Condoleezza Rice should have taken heed, had they only been able to. And by inviting terrorist states like Syria to participate in Annapolis and thereby lavishing credibility upon them, the Americans were only courting disaster. Nor has the situation improved under President Obama whose overtures to the PA, Syria and Iran are just more of the same old hummus, with the difference that it has surrendered not only its intelligence but its dignity. Obama postures that he knows what is best for Israel, just as he knows what is best for America. But the beneficiaries of his wisdom will suffer greatly as they swallow or are force-fed his nostrums and panaceas. When Obama knows what is best, prepare for the worst. In any event, there are lots of bulls rampaging through this particular china shop. The problem is that there are no bullfighters.

This counterproductive peace sham must be put out of its misery and new and different initiatives undertaken. Peace is not achieved between individuals but between governments, and unfortunately the Palestinian Authority is not a unified, competent and trustworthy political entity capable of making and enforcing agreements, as events have proved time and time again. In fact, according to the terms of the Oslo Accords, the PA's official legitimacy lapsed in 1999—the date stipulated for the resolution of the conflict—beyond which date it would have no continuing legal mandate. Besides, what kind of supposedly "moderate" peace partner continues to subscribe to the official Arab boycott of Israel, as does the Palestinian Authority? With regard to the "peace process," we might reverse the old maxim: if it's not fixable, break it—and try something more "creative." These prolonged and anticlimactic negotiations are like a mumblecore film, improvised, scriptless, heavy on verbiage, camera-reliant, bit-part actors pretending to be stars.

In the June 2009 issue of *Commentary*, Hillel Halkin floated the idea of an "Israeli-Palestinian federation" to break the impasse, with Jewish settlers domiciled in Palestine and possessing the same rights as the million-plus Arabs who live in Israel. This will never work. The Jewish settlers would receive neither acceptance not protection from a Palestinian government, which would in any case insist on keeping its state Jew-free. Caroline Glick's "stabilization plan," laid out in the same issue of the magazine, has considerable *theoretical* merit, based as it is on "three pillars" which she defines as: neutralizing external actors, exacting a price for Palestinian terror, and empowering Palestinians as individuals rather than as a collective body manipulated by their leaders. Nevertheless, the problem continues to fester, for how these proposals are to be implemented in the face of Palestinian intransigence and the deeply-rooted terror cult remains an open question. Neither do they indicate how "external actors" like Syria, Hizbullah and Iran are to be 'neutralized" nor do they provide a feasible blueprint for the *actual* construction of a prosperous and viable state committed to peaceful coexistence with Israel.

There is no ideal solution to the Palestinian imbroglio. Some analysts have come to believe that it may be politically expedient to apply a clause of prudential revocation to a peace process that is more process than peace and engage rather in a "mediatorial process" that envisages the return of the Gaza Strip to Egypt, though Hamas would first have to be routed and disbanded; and, after scrubbing the area of its indigenous terror cells, the judicious division of the West Bank between Israel and Jordan. After all, Gaza was Egyptian territory by *force majeure* until 1967 and the West Bank, originally mandated as part of the Jewish "national home" by the League of Nations in 1922, was formally annexed (with British approval) by the Hashemite emirate of Jordan in 1950 after two years of arbitrary rule. In fact, the entire country of Jordan is an afterthought, an artificial entity carved out of the internationally recognized Jewish homeland during the period of the British Mandate. But it is now a geopolitical fact and, as a nation that feels threatened by a zymotic Palestinian enclave, is profoundly involved in an effort to bring political chaos under control. An "independent" Palestine splintered by innumerable factions and with a weak central authority may pose a greater threat to Jordanian security than a closely monitored internal province. It must be admitted, however, that both Egypt and Jordan are reluctant to embrace such an option, and Jordanian authorities have even begun to revoke the citizenship of many thousands of native Palestinians.

The Palestinians, of course, might want to get their act together to forestall the possibility, remote as it may now appear, of one day being re-absorbed by their Arab neighbours. West Bankers might recall the trauma of the seventies when their citizen predecessors were under fire and nearly three thousand of them were killed by the Jordanians, thanks to Arafat's Black September hijinks. And Gazans should remember that the previous generation suffered so terribly under Egyptian rule, experiencing curfews, military conscription, censorship, imprisonment and extortion, that on March 10, 1962 none other than Radio Mecca broadcast a protest.

The other possible solution is to deal with the Palestinian fiscal sinkhole by offering a substantial, one-time, start-up gift to the Palestinian Authority and then cut the purse strings, to the great relief of the Western taxpayer. The responsibility would lie with the Palestinian leaders, with technical assistance from the West if required, to establish a viable economy and a stable social structure, in effect, to grow up. Should the money continue to disappear into weapons purchases, redundant salaries, terrorist infrastructure and private pockets, "Palestine" would have to be declared a failed experiment and a lost cause and abandoned to its own devices. Should military action then become necessary to prevent the formation of a Taliban-type rogue state, as in Afghanistan recently or in Gaza today, it would have to be undertaken vigorously and resolutely to clear the ground for what might eventually emerge as a civil society.

As far as I can tell, these are the only two workable options before us; anything else is self-deception and a prospectus for perpetual discord and endless suffering.

5

Pallywood: A Mirage in the Desert

The *Small Dictionary of Middle East Stereotypes* posted online by the Metula News Agency is not far south of the truth when it defines "Palestine" as "A small piece of paper stuck on Arab maps and atlases to hide Israel." The Palestinian fiction has even been admitted by the Palestinians themselves. In a 1956 speech to the United Nations, Arab League ambassador and founder of the PLO, Ahmed Shukari, declared that "such a creature as Palestine does not exist at all. This land is nothing but the southern portion of Greater Syria." And in a 1977 interview with the Dutch newspaper *Trouw*, Zahir Muhse'in of the PLO Executive Committee confirmed that "The Palestinian people does not exist. The creation of a Palestinian state is only a means for continuing our struggle against the state of Israel for our Arab unity…Only for tactical reasons do we speak today about the existence of a Palestinian people, since Arab national interests demand that we posit the existence of a distinct 'Palestinian people' to oppose Zionism."

Hollywood, too, has contributed to the fiction. Director Paul Haggis' anti-war film, *In the Valley of Elah*, locates the contest of David and Goliath in Palestine, *when no such entity existed.* Haggis may have been ignorant of his biblical history, but his well-known leftish inclinations suggest a specific design at work. It is highly appropriate that *In the Valley of Elah* was filmed in Hollywood, an illusion factory that is about as "real" as Palestine. It is no exaggeration to suggest that the concept of "Palestine," the simulacrum of the "Palestinian," is, when all is said and done, not much more than a Tinseltown movie, an empty fabrication—the historical grounding is absent and the sense of a cohesive national identity has been artificially generated by a political cabal working in tandem with the international media. The fact of the matter is, to adapt a current catch phrase, that the Palestinians are all keffiyeh and no sheep.

The same applies to the Palestinian Authority itself, a crypto-political construct, invented with the collusion of the West and with Arab backing, that has *necessarily* proven incapable of governing, controlling its bellicose factions and creating the conditions for peace and normal civil life. The irony of the situation is especially mordant: the chief obstacle to peace is the very institution that was formed to facilitate its accomplishment. A synthetic contrivance improvised in Oslo, *it has in the current circumstances no alternative but failure*. In point of fact, Jordan is the only visible nation state of the Arabs of Greater Palestine, problematic as it may be. Let us remember once again that when Britain defied the terms of the League of Nations in 1923 and created the protectorate of Jordan from the territory earmarked for Israel, it artificially established a *de facto* Palestinian state which the West Bank was never intended to be a part of. And when the United Nations proposed its 1947 partition plan, further dividing up the Israeli allodium, it was rejected by the Arabs who responded shortly afterward by launching a massive attack against the fledgling Jewish state. Implausible as this may sound in the present circumstances, *another* Palestinian state in one shape or another may come to exist one day, but I suspect it would prove to be little more than the result of a process of political taxidermy.

Certainly, there is no usable template in the rest of the Muslim Middle East to serve as a pattern for emergent statehood—even Turkey, the presumed beacon state, remains unstable. The Palestinian mirage suffers from an even more debilitating version of the Arab debacle which, as the Lebanese-American scholar Fouad Ajami points out in *The Dream Palace of the Arabs*, derives from the connate failure of Arab society in absorbing democratic values and incorporating the principles of the modern nation state. The problem, I would suggest, is that in the Arab mindset, there is no *tertium quid* or intermediate structure between the tribe, which commands the practical loyalty of the individual, and the *ummah*, which invokes a mystical allegiance to the farflung Islamic collective. The nation state is neither one nor the other, too dispersed and abstract an arrangement to create a sense of intimate union, and yet insufficiently numinous and "spiritual" to bind the individual to the transcendent body of the people. Until this changes—which is highly doubtful—the Arab "state" will remain an jerrybuilt contraption to be exploited in the interests of the ruling tribe or family and is thus condemned to be perennially mercurial. We see a similar dilemma in Africa, with the signal difference that the second or transcendent pole is lacking.

Indeed, what Albert Camus said of Algeria in his 1958 *Actuelles III*, that it was only a "virtual nation," is *mutatis mutandis* true of "Palestine"—as it is, for that matter, of Iraq. The latter is not a real nation but three tribal regions, or Ottoman vilayets, cobbled together in the aftermath of the First World War and now, predictably, sinking into a quicksand bog of internal strife and indiscriminate slaughter. At best it will be a magpie nation, assembled from disparate materials, always threatening to come asunder, and held together, if at all, by American strength of will and concrete support. It may manage to survive, as has Algeria, but, politically, it will remain an active volcano. Camus' skepticism of "Arab demands" and raw emotionalism applies equally to "Palestine," which is not a genuine nation but an internally riven enclave of competing jihadist cliques that will likely prove incapable of unified and constructive self-government. It does not take much in the way of aculeate insight to arrive at this conclusion; it is a bit like predicting the past. In the circumstances, it would be foolhardy to dismiss the Shakespearian adage from *Henry VI, Part 3*, "that Beggars mounted, run their Horse to death."[5]

The idea of a two-state solution to the Middle East quandary may well be inherently unworkable. To begin with, many Palestinians are not interested in a two-state solution to their predicament. Palestinian political behaviour and a myriad of polls and studies strongly indicate that the majority of Palestinians do not want a state of their own alongside a Jewish state—to take only one example, a poll conducted in July 2000 showed that 83% of respondents supported Arafat's rejection of the Camp David proposals. The terror cartels, sponsored by Hamas and Fatah, have made it abundantly clear that their agenda is the complete eradication of Israel. The Hamas Covenant, or *Mithaq*, declares that "Israel will exist only until Islam destroys it" and the Fatah charter pledges that "Our struggle will not cease until the Zionist state is entirely eliminated." The only difference between the two is that the latter is more flexible in its strategy, pursuing not the thunderbolt policy of Hamas but the roadmap to serialized conquest. Hamas, like Iran, wishes to obliterate Israel militarily, Fatah to dismember it through negotiations, one Israeli concession at a time. For Fatah, Israel need not be reduced to ashes but annihilated bit by bit in all its aspects—economic, political, martial, demographic and cultural—which is precisely the goal that would be attained by the creation of that increasingly popular chimera, a "single bilateral state." This program should be seen for what it is, a rejuvenated version of Yasser Arafat's "strategy of slices" or "phases," originally recommended by Tunisian president Habib Bourguiba and by Mohammed Heikal, the influential editor of the Egyptian newspaper *Al Ahram*. True, the embryonic Wasatia party, founded by Muhammad Dajani of the American Studies Institute at al-Quds University, does recognize Israel's right to exist, but it is, unfortunately, only a splinter group with little impact on Palestinian public policy or opinion.

Prominent intellectuals as well have abandoned the two-state policy. Leila Farsakh, an assistant professor at the University of Massachusetts, has published an article in the Palestinian advocacy site *The Electronic Intifada*, reprinted in *Le monde diplomatique* for March 7, 2007, blaming stalled negotiations on "Israeli apartheid" and opting for a "one-state solution." Her position is by no means anomalous; it is widely shared by many of her peers and colleagues, both in the Middle East and the West. In fact, her article merely reprises PLO legal advisor Michael Tarazi's op-ed piece in the *New York Times* for October 4, 2004 in which, speaking in his master's voice, he put paid to the notion of a two-state political settlement and proposed that Israel and the Territories merge into a single state. In an article in *The New York Review of Books* for October 23, 2003, entitled "Israel: The Alternative," Western historian Tony Judt, by now a leading figure in the ideological constituency of the anti-Israeli Left, had already called for the dissolution of Israel, arguing for "a single, integrated, binational state of Jews and Arabs." The proposal makes sense for Judt since, by his lights, Israel is "not just an anachronism but a dysfunctional one." The recently retired Latin Patriarch of Jerusalem, Michel Sabbah, who is of Palestinian origin, has also picked up the cudgels, objecting to Israel as a Jewish state and opting for a "political, normal state for Christians, Muslims and Jews." Sabbah is plainly of one mind with chief Palestinian negotiator Saeb Erekat who, two weeks before the Annapolis peace conference, articulated the position that "no state in the world connects its national identity to a religious identity." Like Erekat, Sabbah had nothing to say about the Palestinian Authority's Basic Law which declares that "Islam is the official religion in Palestine," just as the Constitution of Pakistan establishes Islam as the State religion and Saudi Arabia requires by law that all its citizens be Muslims. Sabbah is equally silent about the totalistic Islamic character of the Muslim state which, unlike Israel, discriminates against Christians and often prevents them from freely practising their religion.

Naturally, in such a single-state scenario as has been proposed, the very real likelihood that those Jews who had not been purged would be marked as dhimmis, does not ruffle the single-stater's serenity. Nor should we discount the possibility that in such a scenario, Jerusalem might well become the new Khartoum and Israelis the "black Muslims" of yet another Darfur. "How anyone in their right mind," marvels Menachem Keller in the essay collection *The Jewish Divide over Israel*, "could believe that…this mooted 'state of all its citizens' would respect the rights of minorities (or of majorities for that matter) is beyond comprehension. People who hold this view are either cynical in the extreme or naïve in the extreme. In the former case they knowingly condemn my family and me to persecution and probable death; in the latter case, they insouciantly and casually condemn us to the same fate."

In the epilogue, the Palestinians would then get their state ready-made, without having to endure the labour of building it for themselves. The Israelis will have done all the work, developing a nonpareil scientific establishment, forging a strong industrial base, devising irrigation techniques to reclaim the desert, draining the malarial marshlands and making world-class discoveries in cybernetics, medical technology and research paradigms. The Palestinians would then inherit what they do not deserve and what they have, up to now, done everything in their power to thwart—and, if their performance in Gaza is any indication, would more than likely run into the ground. It is Israel and not the

Palestinians who, in the words of Josef Joffe (*Foreign Policy*, March 1, 2005), "made democracy and the desert bloom in a climate hostile to both liberty and greenery." (The folk etymology of the term "green line," referring to the armistice lines of 1948, can be discerned by glancing at a satellite image of the Holy Land: where the green ends is Israel, where the ochre begins is Arab-controlled.) My own analysis over the years in which I have studied these issues makes it clear to me that Israeli society may be far from perfect, but that Palestinian society is not even close to being far. We might put it this way: Israel is a land that looks old and works new; Palestine is a land that looks old and doesn't work at all.

Gaza is the Palestinians' trial run, the laboratory in which their state-making experiment is being carried out, but, judging by the outcome thus far, it has been, to put it mildly, a probationary failure. In June 2007, Gaza descended into a condition of out-and-out civil war, with a heavily-armed Hamas imposing military control over the entire area. This new crisis has remade the political reality in the territories, although the fault lines were always obvious. Fatah has accused Hamas of conducting institutional assassinations while Hamas charged Fatah for trying to stir the incendiary broth—that is, when they were not busy denouncing Israel. It is reported that al-Qaeda has at least three different leks operating in Gaza, including the Tawheed and Jihad Brigades specializing in abductions and the Righteous Swords of Islam pledged to the destruction of infrastructure. (The latter issued a fatwa against women appearing unveiled in public and on television, threatening to "behead and slaughter to preserve the spirit and morals of our people.") Even prior to the current mayhem, internet cafés, Christian bookstores, music shops and schools were regularly blown up or shot at in Gaza City in a continuing effort to bring the territory back into the cultural embrace of the 7th century, clan feuds proliferated, kidnappings proceeded apace and fratricidal murders and maimings occurred on an almost daily basis.

The West Bank is a more coherent polity but the signs are troubling there as well: intense political infighting, massive corruption, off-the-scale political patronage, ongoing terrorist activity, gang warfare, incipient rebellion against an inept and aging leadership, a grass roots largely sympathetic to Hamas, and important cities like Ramallah, Nablus, Bethlehem and Hebron controlled by Hamas mayoral administrations. In particular, the tension between Fatah chief Mahmoud Abbas and his own armed militiamen, such as the Aksa Martyrs Brigades, will contribute increasingly to the breakdown of public order and provoke destabilizing cabinet resignations. *Realpolitik* suggests a high probability that the West Bank may also be lost in the not too distant future. "So it goes," in Kurt Vonnegut's phrase from *Slaughter House Five*.

The chances are high that a single state incorporating what is now Israel, assuming the fanciful "bi-national" strategy could ever be implemented, or even a separate, unified "Palestinian state," as unlikely as that would appear at present, would already be stillborn or soon be consumed in violence. For, despite their fitful alliances and ethnologic similarities, the Gaza Strip and the West Bank, as I noted in *The Big Lie*, are really two separate entities, geographically, historically and ideologically—the term "two states" applies only here.[6] In addition, Fatah is a nationalist party whereas Hamas is pan-Islamic, rendering them pretty well immiscible, the Bloods and Crips of the Palestinian street. Should their differences one day be bridged, however, the resulting coalition would be unstable, or would ultimately eventuate in a Hamas-controlled fundamentalist pseudo-polity.

For the time being, the more accurate designation would be "three states"—Israel, Hamastan and Fatahland—projecting a solution which, given geographical compression, water shortages, the nigh-irresolvable tensions that continue to tear the region apart and ingrained Palestinian contumacy, is likely to be no solution at all. For our three states may reduce to two again if Hamas manages to subvert and conquer the West Bank, as is always possible given the political weakness of Fatah, its widespread graft and nepotism, its gangs of unruly gunmen extracting protection money from its own people, its consequent lack of popularity and the absence of an *intrinsic* unifying principle. It has been justly said that Fatah fights for salaries whereas Hamas fights for a cause. No contest. The current renewal of a lucrative aid package to Fatah and the international recognition of its legitimacy as a "moderate" alternative to Hamas may well backfire, as it already has in Gaza. There is a strong probability that the resources being funneled to the former will, as before and *one way or another*, eventually wind up in the coffers and arsenals of the latter. Hamas is not only ruthless but shrewd and we should not put it past its leadership to reconfigure their strategy if the situation warrants, eschew the military option and, as I have suggested, conquer from within by "accepting" reconciliation. Nor should we be surprised if Fatah, hollow to the core, acquiesces.

Apart from this, the Israeli leadership has not understood that in reinforcing Fatah against Hamas, they are only cloistering themselves in the phantasm of an unconditioned peace and strengthening yet another terrorist combine in the process. It was with Israeli transfer funds that Salam Fayaad, the former (and once-again) Prime Minister in the PA government, paid the salaries of Hamas militias and officials. Nor have the Israeli negotiators allowed for the possibility that Mahmoud Abbas may yet seek a reconciliation with Hamas in an effort to patch together still another "unity" government. It has now come to light that a number of salaried Fatah officers were engaged in training the newly-formed Hamas street police force in Gaza. Judging from an interview Abbas gave to a Jordanian newspaper (*Al-Dustur*, February 28, 2008) in which he boasted that Fatah had trained Hizbullah, it would appear that Fatah certainly has the necessary expertise. So much for the "good terrorists." Writing in *Yated Ne'man*, Jonathan Rosenblum put it aphoristically: "Sometimes my enemy's enemy is my enemy."

Applying the airline security principles of BPR (Behavior Pattern Recognition), it is a fair assumption that the Palestinians, imagined as travellers, would be arrested at the airport. It should be obvious by this time that they do not comprise "state material" and that a Palestinian state or statelet will probably never really fly. The only thing that has unified the Palestinian warring factions up to now is a common hatred of Israel and it is only in pursuing their objective to liquidate the Jewish state (and, of course, to ensure the continuation of foreign aid) that they may pool their resources. But a shared hatred propped up by a counterfeit theory of revendication is not a durable bond and the presage for the future, despite the Mecca Agreement, the Saudi-backed "Unity government" and the current Egyptian-sponsored "reconciliation" talks, which *to this date* has predictably proved to be unworkable, could only have been more social and political chaos, as events have made clear.

Yet the conflict between Hamas and Fatah has in many quarters been blamed not on Palestinian intransigence or on the undeniable fact that Fatah and Hamas are incompatible bedfellows (though embracing a similar foreign policy) but on Israel for increasing intra-Palestinian tensions by imposing sanctions on the terrorist government, although this has been an international initiative (chiefly honoured in the breach), and Fatah itself promised in December 2006 to monitor cash smuggling through the Rafah border crossing. The Muslim Public Affairs Committee in the U.K., for example, promotes this cockeyed and self-exculpatory view on its website: "For decades, Israel has been attempting to turn Palestinians against each other. Divide to Conquer. This time Israel appears to succeed" (January 29, 2007). Inevitably, the Palestinians will blame Israel for the civil conflict raging in Gaza. Hamas official Moussa Abu Mazouk has already issued a statement from his Damascus headquarters saying "The Israelis are behind all these events" while, on the same day, Fatah legislator Jamal Abu Rub claimed the IDF was responsible for the fratricidal "atrocities" in Gaza. Ghassan Khatib, a former PA minister, commenting on the slaughter in Gaza, opined: "This is what Israel wants. Israel started the separation between Gaza and the West Bank…"—whatever that may signify. Hamas leader Khaled Mashaal is allotted op-ed space in *The Guardian* (May 30, 2007) to blame Israel (and the U.S.) for "these internal conflicts" (and in another piece for that Palestinian-friendly newspaper on July 5 took aim at the "occupier" rather than the powerful Doghmush clan for the kidnapping of reporter Alan Johnston). The supposedly moderate Fatah, with its superior manpower and financial resources, explains its defeat in Gaza by also playing the Israeli card: embroiled in a war against Israel, it was taken off-guard by Hamas.

Joining the posse, Rashid Khalidi, author of several books on the Middle East and holder of the Edward Said Chair of Middle East

Studies at Columbia University, went on National Public Radio to blame Israel (and the U.S.) for having failed to negotiate with Hamas, so that the Gaza meltdown is "the logical, inevitable, natural result." Tariq Ramadan has added his pennyworth to this rank nonsense, blogging on June 18, 2007 that the "Israeli forces of occupation" were the responsible actors for the carnage in Gaza, having "tried to cause an inter-Palestinian conflict" and drive the Palestinians "to distraction." Then we learn that Israel was actually "a cynical spectator" of this intra-Palestinian mayhem. Which is it? Ramadan concludes: "This strategy is insane, inhuman and intolerable," epithets which would better apply to his own infirm analysis. When in November 2007 an Arafat remembrance day rally erupted in gunfire in Gaza City between Hamas and Fatah with many killed and wounded, including women and children, scarcely a word of condemnation was heard—the perpetrators were obviously puppets dancing on the Israeli string. As for the "international community," it is silent when it should be vocal, vocal when it should be silent.

Who, we may ask, are the real marionettes?

6

Israel: *Carte Noire*

The Palestinians and their Muslim sympathizers have no monopoly on lamebrained Israel-bashing. Even as Hamas was murdering its way to dominance, the Geneva-based World Council of Churches launched a new offensive against the miscalled Israeli "occupation" but had not a word to say on the "Islamist" occupation of Gaza by bloody force and seemed unimpressed by the attempted exodus of Gazans to the safety of the "occupying power," aka Israel. Nor has it alluded to the fact that when Israel offered to open the crossings to allow people access to study, work or medical treatment elsewhere, Hamas fired—in the words of Mahmoud Abbas himself—"on any crossing that was opened so as to close it." The WCC then embarked on a week-long commemoration event, mourning the naqba (the Palestinian "catastrophe" of 1948) in an attempt to delegitimize the Jewish state. Jean Raspail's description of the WCC in his dystopian novel *The Camp of the Saints* does not seem particularly overwrought: "shock-troop pastors, righteous in their loathing of anything and everything that smacked of present-day Western society, and boundless in their love of whatever might destroy it." True to form, it has once again covered itself in shame, co-hosting—along with the Mennonite and Quaker communions—a dinner reception in honour of Iranian tyrant and genocidal advocate Mahmoud Ahmadinejad during the 2008 opening of the UN General Assembly.

Human Rights organizations generally come down hard on Israel in complete ignorance of both local context and historical vectors, as, for example, Grassroots International which not only opposes "the so-called 'war on terror'," but calls for the selective boycotting of Israel and condemns "Israeli attacks on civilians in Gaza"—again, not a word about Hamas, intra-Palestinian strife, religious oppression, weapons smuggling and the daily rocket bombardment of Israeli population centers. Similarly, writing in the *washingtonpost.com*,

Arun Gandhi, grandson of the venerated Mahatma and director of the M.K. Gandhi Institute for Nonviolence, determined that Israel is a "snake pit" and that "Israel and the Jews are the biggest players" in the "modern world['s]...culture of violence"—it appears that al-Qaeda, the Taliban, Hizbullah, the Iranian bomb-in-the-making, the Syrian assassination of democratic Lebanese leaders, the Saudi madrassas advocating jihad in the quest for world domination and the Palestinian cult of death have somehow escaped his attention entirely. (We remember that the celebrated grandfather claimed in the Indian newspaper *Harijan* for June 22, 1940 that future generations would "honour Herr Hitler as a genius, as a brave man, a matchless organizer and much more," advising that Jews practice passive resistance against the Nazis, and who, in a conversation with Louis Fischer recorded in the latter's *The Life of Mahatma Gandhi*, opined that "The Jews should have offered themselves to the butcher's knife.") Arun Gandhi's resignation some weeks later did little to redeem his reputation.

Then there is the American NGO Rebuilding Alliance which rebuilds homes in Gaza destroyed in anti-terror strikes; it does not offer to repair homes and farms in Sderot and other Gaza-belt communities or in Israel's north hit by Kassams, mortar shells and Katyushas. The *Boston Globe* has also weighed in with another of its stellar editorials (June 14, 2007): it first upbraids Israel for imposing a "suffocating occupation" on Gaza in 1967 and then reproaches it for its "unilateral withdrawal" in 2005. (Here, at least, the apocryphal term "occupation" has been dropped post-2005.) The Palestinians are once again absolved of responsibility and shorn of agency in the destruction of their civic life. It's the Israelis, stupid!

There are 200,000 Moroccan "settlers" living in Western Sahara, but this, apparently, does not constitute an occupation. Quite the contrary. The UN passed two resolutions that recognized Western Sahara as under Moroccan control while Amnesty International and Human Rights Watch contented themselves with the term "Moroccan-administered." Chinese "settlers" have overrun Tibet, outnumbering the native inhabitants and subduing an entire nation which has effectively ceased to exist under a policy which the Dalai Lama has called "cultural genocide," but this, apparently, does not qualify as an occupation. On the other hand, there is not a single Israeli living in Gaza—to which Israel supplies fuel, electricity and water although Gaza continues to subject its neighbour to bombardment—but this, apparently, is an occupation of the worst sort. The EU External Relations Commission, Amnesty International, Human Rights Watch (now, it seems, partly Saudi-funded, or about to be), UN officials, the international press, and the Foreign Affairs ministries of many nations are plainly living in a world of their own manufacturing, predicated on the denial of reality and its replacement by a deliberate and skilfully concocted hallucination.

And these are by no means isolated moments in the propaganda offensive against Israel along the entire continuum from the secular to the religious. Writing in *Time Magazine's MidEast Blog* for May 8, 2009, columnist Andrew Lee Butters introduced Pope Benedict XVI's visit to the region with a searing indictment of Israel's presumably oppressive treatment of its Christian population. According to this authority, "the creation of Israel has been a disaster for Christians in the Middle East," who formerly prospered under "the multi-sectarian and tolerant history of Arab and Islamic culture." Indeed, not only is the Israeli "occupation of the West Bank strangling the life out of those Christian communities that are left," but it is also responsible for the "civil war between Muslims and Christians" in Lebanon and the Muslim Brotherhood's terror campaign against the Coptic community in Egypt. The range of Butters' latest access of cognitive dissonance is quite breathtaking and leads us to wonder what he will find to blame Israel for next. Darfur? Zimbabwe? Sri Lanka?.

The *National Geographic*, too, has just joined the paper war against Israel, its June 2009 issue featuring a cover article in which Palestinian Christians are compared to rats trapped in an ever-tightening Israeli cage. Of course, the Crusades, American foreign policy and pro-Israeli Christians also come in for the magazine's righteous wrath while the bloody history and practice of Islamic violence and oppression from the 7th century to the present moment are airbrushed out of the picture. Two other victims of the magazine's vendetta are context and truth. But Israeli Jews are the culprits of choice.

The Methodist Church New England Conference recently convened to advocate divestment from companies doing business in Israel, alleging that Israeli "actions endanger Christians." This, of course, is pure libel. The Christian Arab population in Israel is the only Christian community in the Middle East that need not fear the ravages of ethno-religious cleansing. Consider Gaza, for example, where Hamas and radical Muslim sects are driving Christians from their homes and places of worship. The Salafi subculture, when it is not challenging Hamas for being too moderate and unIslamic, is determined to expel the 2,500 Christians living in the Strip. Individual Christians have been attacked by Muslim gunmen, both the Latin Church and the Rosary Sisters School in Gaza City were torched and looted, followed by the destruction of the YMCA library with its 8,000 books, and the director of the Teacher's Bookshop, run by the Palestinian Bible Society, was stabbed to death. On December 22, 2008, Hamas legalized crucifixion.

Further afield, it is Egypt that has repressed its Coptic Christian minority for generations, Sudan that has closed the Christian Unity High School in Khartoum, Malaysia that has confiscated Christian books on the grounds that they are offensive "to the sensibilities of Muslims" (*washingtonpost.com*), Jordan that has arrested eight Christian evangelicals for "propagating the Christian faith" (*Media Line News Agency*), Algeria that is cracking down on Evangelical churches whose liturgy, in the words of Algerian minister of religious affairs, Bouabdellah Ghlamallah, is equivalent to "terrorism" (*Realite-EU*) and the Shi'a majority in Basra that is killing and abducting Christians, having forced the cancellation of the 2007 Christmas festivities. Catholic churches are frequently bombed in Iraq, the Chaldean Archbishop of Mosul, Paulus Faraj Rahho, was abducted and killed—he was not the first—and on May 21, 2009, a suicide bomber detonated in an Assyrian Christian market in Baghdad, killing 12 people and wounding twice that number. Estimates put the current exodus of Christians from Iraq at over half the Christian population of the country. Very little is said about the imprisonment and extrajudicial killings of Christian converts in Iran, and no official protests have been lodged or media attention paid over the solitary confinement and prosecution in March 2009 of two young Iranian women, Maryam Rustampoor and Marzieh Amirizadeh, for having embraced the Christian faith (*Assyrian International News Agency*). On August 1, 2009 in the Christian villages of Gojra and Koriyan in Pakistan, Muslim mobs set 125 houses on fire and burned eight Christian to death (various newspaper accounts). *None of which has anything to do with Israel* and everything to do with Muslim "sensitivities."

Archbishop of Canterbury Rowan Williams has added his authority to this latest cargo of anti-Israeli archrubbish, claiming that the Israeli security fence, built "*ostensibly* for keeping out the terrorists," is contributing to the decline of the Christian community in the Holy Land (italics mine). Kenneth Woodward, contributing editor of *The Wall Street Journal*, is apparently of the same mind, opining that the Christian community in Bethlehem is being squeezed by "Israel's security wall, its restrictive exit permit system, roadblocks and military checkpoints [that] make it impossible for most Holy Land Christians to visit the shrines…" (December 24, 2007).

But the truth, as is usual in such situations, is the complete opposite. We recall that it was Palestinian gunmen who occupied and defaced the Church of the Nativity in Manger Square. According to the IMIA (International Media Intelligence Analysis) service (September 25, 2007), citing a Christian leader in Nazareth, the Christian community in the West Bank could become extinct within 15 years owing to the systematic persecution led by organizations with links to Mahmoud Abbas. Evangelical pastor Isa Bajalia reported that he was forced by a Fatah security official to flee Ramallah, where he had served his parish for the last sixteen years, for the safety of Jerusalem. Writing in the London daily *Al-Sharq Al-Awsat* (February 2, 2008), Saudi journalist Hussein Shukakshi made no bones about the expulsion and emigration of Christians from Arab lands: "the Arab world is being drained of its Christian residents. The rate of Christian emigration from Lebanon, Jordan, Iraq, Egypt, Palestine, Sudan, and Syria has reached astonishing proportions. Palestine in particular is facing a plan to eradicate the entire deeply-rooted Christian presence from all its territories."

In his column for *Al-Ayyam* (October 25, 2008), Palestinian journalist 'Abd Al-Nasser Al-Najjar arrives at the same conclusion: "Christians are being persecuted…in most Arab countries." In Palestine, "the trend is the same….The most fundamental problem [is that] we continue to instill a horrific culture in our children, one that sees Christians as infidels." Hanna Massad, Pastor of the Gaza Baptist Church, does not mince his words either: "This is ethnic cleansing at its worst" (*Cybercast News Service*). Human rights lawyer Justus Reid Weiner, writing in *IBL News from a Christian View* (December 5, 2007), quotes pastor (and author) Don Finto to the effect that, while receiving civil treatment in Israel, "The Christian community in the Palestinian areas has shrunk to 1.7 percent"—down from its staple 15 percent.

Finto also points out that the Christian population of Bethlehem, once a majority, has decreased by a factor of four to the status of a besieged minority. Bethlehem has now become a dangerous city for West Bank Christians—a fact which has nothing whatsoever to do with Israeli activities. The Vatican is quite aware of this alarming development, having "relocated" the Nativity Scene traditionally displayed in front of St. Peter's Basilica from the manger in Bethlehem to Joseph's carpentry shop in Nazareth and giving as its reason that it was "time for a change." The Church's Muslim assailants will obviously concur with this act of symbolic displacement. According to Vatican officials, there is a textual basis for this decision, namely Matthew 1: 24-25 where we learn that Joseph "took unto him his wife:/and knew her not until she had brought forth her firstborn son…," which suggests the miraculous event may have taken place in Joseph's home city of Nazareth. The learned fathers have obviously not proceeded in their reading of the Scriptures as far as the second chapter of Matthew, verse 1, where we are surprised to discover that "…Jesus was born in Bethlehem…" (The practice of exegetical typology is also put in some jeopardy since the patristic interpretation of the famous passage in Micah 5:2—a "Parenthesis" referring to "the birth and rejection of the King" and collated with various chapters in the Book of Matthew, which tells us that the "ruler in Israel" will come out of Bethlehem—must now be discounted as well.)

What will happen to the Nativity Scene when Nazareth is depopulated of its Christians is another question. Perhaps it can be transferred to Tel Aviv. But the act of sterilization is a widespread phenomenon, abetted by Christian spinelessness and duplicity beyond the borders of this latest Mortality Scene. A Church official told Israeli-Arab reporter Khaled Abu Toameh that "radical Islamic groups are waging a campaign to get rid of us and no one seems to care" (*Jerusalem Post*, December 8, 2007). There is a Christian purge gathering strength across the Arab world. The only Middle Eastern country in which Christians may worship freely is...you guessed it.

Nevertheless, the National Council of Churches in the U.S., like the Anglican Church, blames the Israelis for the plight of Palestinian Christians suffering under the policies of radical Islam and accordingly favours outreach to Muslims. Thus the NCC convened an Ecumenical Study Seminar at the 2007 convention of the Wahhabi-inspired Islamic Society of America in order to—in the words of its Interfaith Relations office—"reflect and learn together." More recently, the NCC has gone out of its way to ingratiate itself to the Islamic fact, responding positively to a Muslim encyclical, entitled "A Common Word Between Us and You" and accepting the appeal to open a dialogue. In so doing, it revealed the depth of its ignorance, plainly unaware of the context framing the invitation, almost to the letter. Koran 3:64 reads: "O People of the Book! Come to common terms as between us and you, that we worship none but Allah." Q.E.D.

Cringing in mortification before the presumed sins of its own "extremist Christians," the Council shut its eyes to the Islamic conquest of much of Europe, the reduction of Constantinople, the 400-year enslavement of Greece, the abduction of young Christians to serve in the janissary corps and the current onslaught against the post-Christian West, including the modern, collective version of the Crucifixion in the Holy Land. None of this should strike us as eccentric when one notes that the NCC, which at one time funded Communist regimes in Poland, Yugoslavia and Nicaragua and considers itself at the forefront of the "religious Left," is financially dependent on organizations of a distinctive leftist orientation like the Sierra Club, the Tides Foundation, George Soros' Open Society

Institute, *MoveOn.org* and especially the Ford Foundation. Equally oblivious to the predicament of its own co-religionists, the Evangelical Lutheran Church in America has recently joined the anti-Israeli coalition, determining to review its "economic options" in Israel and recommending investment in the Palestinian Authority. This is turning the other cheek with a vengeance.

State actors are equally hostile; for example, the Norwegian embassy in Israel, accepting unsubstantiated reports from unfriendly NGOs without clarification, has accused the Israeli government of practicing torture, burying the fact that the world's real torture states are countries like Syria, Egypt and Iran. The animosity toward the Jewish state likewise accounts for the fact that Reporters Without Borders ranked Israel, which enjoys an unrestricted press and generously hosts foreign reporters on its soil, *below* the Palestinian Authority despite frequent kidnappings, harassment and intimidation of journalists, including gunpoint conversions to Islam. Jerusalem has the highest proportion of foreign journalists per capita of any city in the world. The *Boston Globe*, for example, maintains four foreign correspondents: one for Europe (in Berlin), one for South America (in Bogota), and two in Jerusalem for the Middle East—the accommodation is just too good and the stories too easy to exaggerate into slanted, blockbuster news events.

As far as honest reporting of Israel's predicament goes, it has been said that these journalists limit their coverage until more Israelis are killed, true to their operating precept: "If it bleeds, it leads." The majority of foreign journalists on the scene rely on Palestinian stringers for their information and do not wish to alienate their sources, so that the reports they file scarcely differ from covert propaganda for Hamas and Fatah. And what will our news organs say now as Gaza plunges ever more deeply into self-engendered chaos? A purely rhetorical question. These journalists were predictably furious when Israeli officials closed the Kerem Shalom crossing into Gaza on November 14, 2008, after 60 kassams and 20 mortars had pummeled southern Israel. Strangely, not one of these offended reporters turned their ire on Hamas for bringing the situation about or considered re-locating to Egypt and entering Gaza from there.

Canadian newspapers are not well represented in correspondents to the area, but this has not prevented many of the more influential dailies from parroting the anti-Israeli line. Canada's largest newspaper, the *Toronto Star*, is practically indistinguishable from London's *Independent* and *Guardian. Globe and Mail* columnist Rick Salutin has struck the note of bleeding-heart sympathy for the Palestinian cause that we detect almost everywhere in the collaborationist media. According to this political savant, the Palestinians appear to be largely innocent of the pandemonium they have unloosed. They linger in poverty and deprivation because they have been refused "their money," although as we have seen little of this money is "theirs" to begin with, and the cash pipeline continues to flow and to be turned into weaponry and numbered accounts. Next we learn that the Palestinians "tried the democratic route and were treated with contempt..." (June 16, 2007). Salutin is apparently referring to the election of a thugocratic party that proceeded to impose its will by intimidation and violence, that maintains close ties with the world's militant theocracies, that wishes to transform Gaza into a jihadist state and a base for global terrorism, that has moved to restore shari'a law, that is terrorizing and expelling its Christian citizens and that has engaged in a war against Israel, launching rockets regularly into the southern Negev. "What can you say," he asks ingenuously. What we can say is that such maudlin and abject pandering to an Islamofascist enemy by the Salutins of this world will one day come back to haunt them. At some point in the future they will be touched personally by the violence they have condoned. The backflush is inevitable: it is only a question of time. For there is no silver lining in a clouded judgment.

And the farce shows no sign of abating, especially in the U.K. which, as Melanie Phillips has documented in her book *Londonistan*, her website and sundry articles, has effectively gone over to the other side. Shortly before the renewed havoc in Gaza, Britain's National Union of Journalists in its annual delegates meeting called for sanctions against Israel for its "savage, pre-planned attacks on Lebanon" and its "slaughter of civilians in Gaza." (It took three months for the Union leadership, realizing the untenableness of a syndicate sworn to impartiality actually taking sides in a conflict, to revoke its decision.) But, once again, the truth was stood completely on its head in the interests of a coarse and obscene ideology. And the truth in this case is so obvious as to be almost obstreperous: the Lebanese summer war of 2006 was caused by Hizbullah's unprovoked aggression across internationally recognized boundaries; Iran and Syria are manipulating such events in a concerted plan to destabilize the region; Gazans are being "slaughtered" by their own militias; Israeli civilians in Sderot and other border communities are subject to constant Palestinian rocket and mortar attacks; no foreign journalist has ever been kidnapped in Israel although this is a frequent occurrence in Gaza in which, officially, 22 journalists have to date been abducted, though the number is probably higher (the most conspicuous recipient of Gazan hospitality, BBC correspondent Alan Johnston, was held in captivity for months); and—a delicious irony—the very laptops on which these gazetteers type their lying reports are crammed with Israeli-made components. Nor did the NUJ have any anything to say about the use of a vehicle marked as a TV-news van by Palestinian Islamic Jihad and al-Aqsa Martyrs Brigades in an attempt to kidnap Israeli soldiers near the Kissufim Crossing on June 9, 2007. To this day, the NUJ has not uttered the slightest protest over the kidnapping of Hafez Asakreh, a reporter working for the Ma'an news agency in Bethlehem, by Palestinian gunmen. "They wanted us to publish unfounded stories," Asakreh explained upon his release. It is also equally silent on the arrest of journalists by PA security forces in the West Bank as it is on the fact that only Hamas-approved journalists are permitted to operate in the Gaza Strip. In November 2007, seven Palestinian journalists were beaten and arrested by Hamas and Fatah security forces, but we would not have heard of this had we relied on the Union for information. Nor has it commented on the expulsion of internationally accredited Israeli journalists from the premises of the Saudi Arabian embassy on the eve of the Annapolis peace conference while journalists from other countries were allowed to remain.

The NUJ has been at it again, marching in Trafalgar Square on May 16, 2009 arm in arm with the Palestine Solidarity Campaign, the British Muslims Initiative, The Palestine Forum in Britain and other such groups—this during a week in which another 1,000 people were killed in Sri Lanka, hundreds killed and millions were displaced in sectarian violence in Pakistan, the detention of Aung San Suu Kyi by the military junta in Burma was extended, the centrifuges were spinning at the Natanz nuclear facility in Iran, and the situation in Zimbabwe and Darfur continued to worsen. Which only goes to show how ignorance has been institutionalized and that antisemitism is not only a kind of autonomic psychosis but is also somehow *willed.* (Unless, as I have speculated elsewhere, there is something like an antisemitism molecule bred into the gene puddles of these impostors.)

The meld of stark hypocrisy, deliberate blindness and cultivated stupidity, this kind of snuff journalism, among those who should know better given their opportunities for professional surveillance, indicates, to use the NUJ's own words, a "savage, pre-planned attack" on *Israel*. But this is an old story, where, as Jonathan Frankel showed in *The Damascus Affair: 'Ritual Murder,' Politics, and the Jews in 1840*, the European press in particular is only following in the footsteps of its 19th century precursor that helped to inflame the notorious "Damascus affair" in which Jews were, once again, subjected to the blood libel. Recent events in Iran, following the rigged elections and popular violence of June 2009, should perhaps have predisposed all reasonable journalists—certainly there must be three of four such specimens lurking in the corridors of the NUJ—to rethink their biases. But such reconsideration was left to the slightly less demeritorious Jean-François Julliard, secretary general of Reporters Without Borders, who went on AP Television News in Paris to draw attention to the fate of the ten or more journalists who had been arrested by the regime. It should also be noted that no journalist, no matter how critical or mendacious, has been arrested in Israel.

Not to be outclassed, a gang of British doctors has since called for the World Medical Association to boycott Israeli physicians, basing their demand on a false interpretation of the Fourth Geneva Convention, citing provisions that do not exist in the Convention, and ignoring the Palestinian use of medical vehicles to facilitate terror attacks on Israeli civilians. Also absent was any reference to the fact that Palestinian "fighters" use hospital grounds and rooftops as either staging points or targets in their own intramural battles—and no statement was issued when on June 9, 2007 a certain Dr. Fayez al-Barrawi was kidnapped by Fatah "militants" from his northern Gaza hospital, shot five times and dumped in the street. As of this writing these British doctors have had nothing to say about the firing of scores of physicians by Hamas or the arrest of Dr. Duhni al-Wahidi, head of the Gaza Physicians Syndicate.

Shortly afterward, the University and College Union jumped aboard the boycott train, reviving the call for a boycott of Israeli universities and academics and for "a moratorium on research and cultural collaboration with Israel"—a move fostered by pressure groups like the anti-Zionist Socialist Workers Party and the anti-Zionist Stop the War Coalition. The UCU-Left, another core boycott group, succeeded in blocking a membership ballot on the issue. It is telling to note that the Union was silent on the Gaza infighting which led to the closure of universities and the suspension of final examinations for university and high school students, and has since remained mum on the anarchy is Gaza. It has not commented on the fact that many Palestinian universities host student branches of Hamas, Islamic Jihad and other terrorist groups. Nor has it acknowledged the setting ablaze of Al Quds Open University by Hamas, the virtual destruction of the Islamic University in Gaza by Fatah, the forced cancellation by Fatah gunmen of matriculation exams in Nablus, the subsequent closing of Bir Zeit University in the West Bank to avoid clashes between students of rival parties, the brawl erupting at Al Najah University in Nablus between rival Fatah-and Hamas-aligned factions in which one student was shot dead and three wounded, the inculcation of jihadist doctrine and recruitment of potential suicide bombers across the many Muslim campuses in the territories, etc. In late November 2007, studies were again suspended and students evacuated at Bir Zeit when clashes flared between supporters of Fatah and the Marxist-oriented Popular Front for the Liberation of Palestine. Members of the PFLP had attacked a Fatah student, driving nails into his feet, whereupon Fatah irregulars appeared on campus unleashing the usual mayhem. The Union remained silent. In April 2008, studies were suspended at Al-Azhar University in Gaza City and Hebron University in the West Bank owing to factional infighting between Hamas-and Fatah-affiliated student gangs. The Union remained silent. Despite the transparent disclaimer that the Union's anti-Israeli and pro-Palestinian activities are not directed against Jews, it is obvious that the watchword term "academic freedom," used to justify its assembly motions, is only cryptograph for "antisemitism" and now serves as camouflage for the *intellectual apartheid* increasingly practised by the "knowledge community."

And such intellectual dishonesty does not stop there. One remarks that the Union did not see fit to pronounce on the Iranian crackdown on higher education (which Mahmoud Ahmadinejad has called "the second great Islamic cultural revolution," after Ayatollah Khomeini's initial closure of the universities), the growing blacklist of authors and books, the notorious Ashura Brigade campus police force or the thousands of university students who have been expelled, imprisoned or "disappeared." It had nothing to say about the disturbing fact that British universities, with the approval of the Foreign Office, have admitted sixty Iranian students, to supplement the thirty already in place, into advanced nuclear physics programs and other "proliferation-sensitive" courses (*Sunday Times*, October 28, 2007)—which seems to this observer a far more serious threat to Western security interests than the activities of integrated and peaceable Israeli universities. (The Netherlands, at least, according to a report from *Agence France-Press* for July 5, 2008, has caught on, banning Iranian students from studying nuclear technology.)

That the union administration ultimately decided to back away from their boycott strategy after seeking "legal advice" and being informed that a boycott would be illegal, amounts to little more than a face-saving gesture. The intention was clear, the sentiment remains unchanged, and the notion of "legality," which should anyway have been explored prior to the "initiative," is both irrelevant in the broader circumstances of anti-Jewish feeling and trivial in the light of professional morality. The legal check, however, did not stop the UCU from trying again. On March 29, 2008, the Union leadership voted once more, with the approval of the Deans Association, to include a motion for its next Conference to boycott all Israeli educational institutions. Meanwhile, not a word of protest about the dismissal of hundreds of teachers in Gaza for "political reasons" at the beginning of the 2008/2009 school year. Recently as well, the general union of the London School of Economics narrowly lost a motion, by just seven votes, proposed by the International Solidarity Movement to boycott Israel which it calls a xenophobic and racist state.

Such intellectual apartheid would include the "arts community" as well: the Tate Museum has tarnished its mandate by rejecting submissions of Jewish Israeli artists to its exhibition of Middle Eastern Art while accepting the works of Arab Israeli artists and replacing the designation "Israel" by "Palestine." And London's Royal Court Theatre appears to have gone into the business of demonizing Israel as well, hosting such one-sided, propagandistic plays as *My Name is Rachel Corrie* co-written by *Guardian* editor Katherine Viner, and *Seven Jewish Children: A Play for Gaza*, billed as a "ten minute history of Israel," written by Caryl Churchill, a patron of the Palestine Solidarity Campaign. While not scrupling to stage crudely anti-Israeli works that cater to the antisemitic sentiment permeating British public and cultural life, the theater's associate director Ramin Gray admitted that he would be reluctant to stage a play critical of Islam. One can readily imagine the public outcry, complete with street demonstrations and acts of violence, had the play been titled *Seven Muslim Children*. It is also noteworthy that Churchill's play is not called *Seven Israeli Children* but *Seven Jewish Children*!

A coalition of British architects seem to feel the same way, including the president and president-elect of the Royal Institute of British Architects, signing a petition in *The Guardian* accusing their Israeli counterparts of collaborating in the "social, political and economic oppression of Palestinians." This is a rickety argument entirely without foundations, although one may wonder to what extent the plum contracts associated with the construction of London's proposed mega-mosque may contribute to such unwarranted allegations. Add to this the fact that much of London's prestige real estate is in Arab hands and the picture grows even clearer. Profit and Jew-hatred make for a powerful brace of motives.

Refusing to be left behind in the stampede to isolate Israel, UNISON, the largest trade union in the U.K., then adopted its own "economic, cultural, academic and sporting boycott," followed by the British Transport and General Workers Union whose Birmingham branch secretary, Eric McDonald, shamelessly indulged in the Israel/Nazi aspersion. And let's not forget the U.K. registered charities, such as the NGO War on Want whose mandate is "fighting global poverty." Instead it has devoted its time and resources to demonizing Israel, campaigning to have the security barrier dismantled, sanctions imposed, the Israel-Europe trade agreement annulled and the Palestinian naqba recognized during Holocaust Remembrance Day. In so doing, it has radically simplified the historical background to the regional conflict and assembled a raft of distorted and misleading statistics to support its vendetta. Like most people, War on Want does not know that the term "naqba" was not coined by the Palestinians in 1948, but was introduced by the Lebanese political writer and Arab nationalist George Antonius in 1920. It referred to the outrage felt by Palestinian Arabs at being separated from their Syrian homeland by colonial diplomacy after the First World War. The term was later appropriated by their descendants who had refused to accept the 1947 UN partition of the land into two separate states, with dire consequences of their own making.

Another British Union has now thrown in its lot with its compeers. In August 2009, the Fire Brigades Union turned its attention from extinguishing fires to extinguishing Israel, which it considers the most burning issue of all, calling for a total boycott of the country.

The University, too, has once again entered the lists. A typical example is furnished by the Oxford Union which, inaugurating a debate on the Israeli/Palestinian quagmire, named among the anti-Israeli panel the zealous revisionist historians and single-state proponents Avi Shlaim and Ilan Pappe while selecting the self-hating Jew and admirer of Holocaust-denier David Irving, Norman Finkelstein, *to represent the pro-Israeli side of the topic*! Reacting to criticism, the debating society replaced Finkelstein with Peace Now U.K. co-chair Paul Usiskin. After unsuccessfully demanding that Finkelstein be re-instated, Shlaim and Pappe withdrew from the debate along with their confederate, Palestinian activist Ghadi Karmi, forcing cancellation of the event. The Union, however, then invited Irving to participate in a future debate. It has recently concluded yet another on the motion "This House believes that the state of Israel has a right to exist," with Ilan Pappe and Ghadi Karmi arguing against and noted Israel-haters Norman Finkelstein—again—and philosopher Ted Hondrich *arguing for*. (In article for *CounterPunch*, October 25, 2003, Hondrich compared the Palestinians to the Jews in the Warsaw Ghetto and claimed that "the Palestinian suicide bomber does have a moral right to her act of terrorism.") Finkelstein, who has since come out in support of Hizbullah, then voted against the motion that he had nominally agreed to defend. Let us not be deceived. These are only "scholars" in hoodies, practicing the art of swarming.

No surprise here. The history of British antisemitism goes back a long way. The "blood libel" against the Jews began in Norwich in 1144 and Jews were evicted wholesale from Britain in 1290, two centuries before the Spanish Expulsion. Although the Balfour Declaration recognized a Jewish homeland in the Middle East, the British soon reneged on their commitment, restricting Jewish immigration, arming the Arab militias and permitting Sir John Glubb to lead the Arab Legion in its war against the newly-founded Jewish state. It would be sheer folly to expect high moral conduct from the British intelligentsia who have distinguished themselves over many generations as traitors to their country (the Oxford Union once declared "This house shall not fight for King and Country"), communist fellow travellers, Secret Service moles and pro-Arab agitators, so that George Orwell typed them as "an island of dissident thought."

Just as worrisome, England is home to 1.5 million Muslims, nearly half of whom live in London. The demographics are compelling. Britain's military commander in Afghanistan, Brigadier Mark Carleton-Smith, made waves recently when he said that the war against the Taliban in Afghanistan cannot be won; closer to the truth, I would surmise, is that the war against radical jihad and Islamic infiltration in Britain cannot be won. An issue of the hip London weekly *Time Out* features an article titled "Is London's Future Islamic," and urges the "advantages [Islam] would bring across a wide range of areas in the future," including a moratorium on alcohol, tighter abs (the act of praying five times a day "is designed to keep worshippers fit…their stomachs trim"), a reduction in obesity through a halal diet, control of the hospital superbug owing to the ritual washing of hands and feet, an increase in public green spaces and, of all things, inter-faith accommodation. London, we are told, in the face of the evidence streaming in from every quarter of the globe, "would become a little less cruel."

It is not clear whether the article was intended satirically—the framing context does not yield enough information to justify it unequivocally as satire—but people really believe this garbage. As does, apparently, the senior prelate of the Church of England himself. In a BBC interview on January 4, 2008, Rowan Williams argued in favour of recognizing certain aspects of shari'a law, which in any case "seems unavoidable," and that Muslims should not have to choose between "the stark alternatives of cultural loyalty or state loyalty." Indeed, many already don't. There are now many shari'a courts operating in Britain—according to Damian Thompson writing in *The Telgraph.co.uk* for June 29, 2009, perhaps as many as 85—in cities such as London, Birmingham, Rotherham and Dewsbury, with several *officially* adopted in London, Birmingham, Barford, Manchester and Nuneaton, and two more sanctioned for Glasgow and Edinburgh. (This policy brings to mind a scene from Raspail's *The Camp of the Saints* in which the Archbishop of Paris, helpless before the multitudes of immigrants and foreigners, turns over thirty churches to the city's Grand Mufti to be converted into mosques.) Williams has now established himself as a leading Western proponent of what has come to be known as "shari'a creep." Although this latest scandal has earned Williams an international reputation for episcopal waywardness, the writing was already on the Church wall. Interviewed earlier in the Islamic magazine *Emel* (35), Williams skipped over the bloody deeds of the homegrown, British-Muslim terrorist gangs, the Taliban in Afghanistan, the Ba'athists in Iraq and the Palestinian terrorists and suicide bombers the better to condemn the United States for acting as a "chosen nation" and Israel for causing "colossal" suffering among the Palestinians. Islam received only the mildest of reproofs, namely, that its "present political solutions aren't always very impressive," but the interview is saturated with discreet flattery. (Williams had to swallow a dram of his own medicine when, to his dismay, the BBC appointed a Muslim, Aaqil Ahmed, as head of religious broadcasting.)

Ditto Prince Charles, considering his many favourable pronouncements on the status of Islam and his intention, according to a letter leaked to the *Daily Telegraph*, to revise on his accession to the throne the monarchical title "defender of the faith" to "defender of faith" with the added rubric "and defender of the Divine." Islam, intones the Prince, "can teach us today a way of understanding and living in the world which Christianity itself is poorer for having lost" (*Middle East Quarterly*, September 1997). In a much-quoted passage of *The Decline and Fall of the Roman Empire*, Edward Gibbon speculated on the future course of history had Charles Martel lost the battle of Tours-Poitiers in 732 C.E.: "the Arabian fleet might have sailed without a naval combat into the mouth of the Thames. Perhaps the interpretation of the Koran would now be taught in the schools of Oxford and her pulpits might demonstrate to a circumcised people the sanctity and truth of the revelation of Mahomet." The "Saracens" might even have penetrated to "the highlands of Scotland." "From such calamities, "he concludes, "was Christendom delivered by the genius and fortune of one man." As a glance at the daily newspaper would confirm, an analogous calamity has now befallen the shores of Albion and Caledonia, thanks to the lack of genius and misfortune of multitudes. What we seem to be observing is an uncanny re-enactment of the British love affair with the Ottomans in the latter part of the 19th century.

From the viewshed of this breed of neo-Muslim flunkeys, it would seem that Islam outperforms Anglicanism by a wide margin. But the British disease is highly contagious and the ideological superbug is on the verge of causing a world-wide influenza, aided by a false (anti-Western) diagnosis and the wrong (anti-Israeli) prescription. As an illustration of the latter, on October 28, 2008, former Iranian president Mohammad Khatami was invited to address the University of Freiburg in Germany. That Khatami had referred to Zionism as a "continuation of fascism" and portrayed Israel as "an incurable wound on the body of Islam…that really possesses demonic, stinking, contagious blood" was of little concern to his hosts. (Freiburg was the intellectual home of philosopher and Nazi sympathizer Martin Heidegger, whom Hitler had appointed Rector.)

But it seems to start in the U.K. Under a loophole in Britain's Universal Jurisdiction Law exploited by Muslim activists and their sympathizers, a warrant was issued against retired Israeli general Doron Almog for war crimes; Almog avoided arrest by remaining on his plane at Heathrow airport. Public Security Minister Avi Dichter and Brigadier-General Aviv Kochavi decided to cancel their trips to Britain to avoid the wrath of British Home Secretary Jacqui Smith. Transport Minister Shaul Mofaz and former IDF Chief of Staff Moshe Ya'alon have met with similar difficulties. Again, in March of 2008 the UK's Home Office banned Moshe Feiglin, a member of Israel's Likud Party's central committee, from entering the country on the grounds that his opinions were an incitement to violence, though Feiglin had not applied for a visa and had no intention of visiting the U.K. Yet a few days earlier, the Home Office granted entry to Hizbullah's Al-Manar TV news editor, Ibrahim Mousawi, who had broadcast a 29-part documentary accusing Jews of conspiring to world domination and alleged that Israel was responsible for 9/11. That Moussawi had also aired a program depicting Jews sugaring off the blood of a young Christian victim to make Passover matza was obviously deemed irrelevant. While maintaining its ban on important Israeli figures, the Ms. Smith once again approved Moussawi's entry into the country on November 2008.

Ms. Smith, however, is no paragon of virtue herself. Embarrassed by leaks to the Press revealing that she had claimed parliamentary expenses for several adult videos rented by her husband, she thought it prudent to step down prior to the June 2009 Labour Party Cabinet shuffle. As Winston Churchill said in a speech to the House of Commons on November 16, 1948, "The English never draw a line without blurring it."

And so it is. In August 2009, Ms. Smith's successor as Home Secretary welcomed the hate-spewing Saudi cleric Sheikh Abdul Rahman al-Sudais, who calls Jews "rats of the world," considers Christians "cross worshippers" and slanders Hindus as "idol worshippers." Nor to this date has the ban against prominent Israeli public figures been revoked.

Ms. Smith and her kind may be rather shady characters but they are absolutely clear about where they stand when it comes to Jews. And so we are back, in a way, where we began—not, perhaps, kicking Jews out, but, certainly with regard to designated Israeli officials, keeping them out. This is one line that is not yet blurred.

7

Strike Three or Ball Four?

The feral antipathy towards Israel, the concerted bid to leverage it out of the community of nations, accounts for the obstinate reluctance on the part of Western academics, intellectuals, professionals, churchmen and journalists to examine the *true history* of the region, which would expose the Palestinian claim to plenary proprietorship as largely fraudulent while buttressing the Jewish and Israeli title to rightful occupancy. As Joan Peters has shown in her scrupulously researched seven-year study *From Time Immemorial*, examining census reports and internal memoranda during the British Mandate, perhaps a majority of the "original" Palestinian inhabitants were relative newcomers to the territory in dispute, having migrated into the Holy Land from the surrounding Arab countries, mainly from what was then known as Greater Syria (i.e., Syria and Lebanon) when still part of the Ottoman empire, and afterwards during the post-Balfour period. Analogously, the Reverend James Parkes, in *Whose Land? A History of the Peoples of Palestine*, has built a powerful case for the Jewish, not the Palestinian, hereditament. His thesis has been recently strengthened by genetic research which has corroborated the provenance of Jews from the Middle East, basing its conclusions on the recently discovered DNA signature, called the Cohen Modal Haplotype, pointing toward a common ancestor dating back to the time of Aaron and Moses, circa 1000 B.C.E. (See also, among many such studies, the *American Journal of Human Genetics*, 2003, treating of Y-chromosome evidence for the origin of Ashkenazi Levites.)

As for the national collectivity we refer to as "Palestine," it does not exist. There is, rather, a phenomenon we may call "Palestinianism," a historically recent political movement rooted in hatred of Israel, palpable antisemitism, constructed memory and the Islamic summons to territorial conquest. No settlement in the land of Israel, with the possible exception of Ramla, has a name that indicates Arab extraction—they are mostly of Hebrew origin with a sprinkling of Greek and Latin, covered up at a later time with Arab appellations. There was not even a Palestinian national anthem until one was hastily dreamed up at the onset of the 1987 Intifada. In an Internet letter posted on November 6, 2002, Yashiko Sagamori asks "a few basic questions" about this imaginary Palestinian country: *inter alia*, "When was it founded and by whom? What were its borders? What was its form of government? Was Palestine ever recognized by [another] country? What was the name of its currency? (Today, it is the Israeli shekel.) And finally, since there is no such country today, what caused its demise and when did it occur?" Sagamori might have added the definitive fact that *there is no such thing as a "Palestinian" archeology* though the Holy Land is rich with sites and monuments that testify to a long and continuous Jewish presence. As Bernard-Henri Levy remarks in *Left in Dark Times*, "This supposedly decisive Palestine is nothing more than a geographic reference, a very uncertain place name, a signifier at most."

The historical record conclusively shows not only that there was never any such thing as a Palestinian nation but also that there is no Palestinian *ethnicity*—in the sense that there is a Jewish or Tibetan ethnicity—and that *there was no coherent political grouping known as "Palestinians" until after the 1967 war.* A Palestinian entity was only recognized by the Arab countries at the 1974 Rabat Summit Conference. (Although the Palestinian Liberation Organization was founded in 1964—*before there were any "Territories" to be "liberated"*—it was largely an Egyptian affair controlled by Gamel Abdel Nasser.) 1967 is the founding year of the hypothesis now known as "Palestine." What we call "Palestinian history" has just celebrated its forty-second birthday! The designation "Palestinians" was not in official use under the Ottoman imperium and the British applied the term *only to the Jewish inhabitants* of the region. Local Arabs rejected the term "Palestine" and pressed for "Southern Syria" and even "Iraq." Eli Hertz, president of Myths and Facts Inc., points out that the Territories "are filled with families named Elmisri (Egyptian), Chalabi (Syrian), Mugrabi (North Africa)"; and Habash, the surname of arch-terrorist George Habash, originates in Ethiopia (*MythsandFacts.com*, May 16, 2008). Unlike the original Jewish inhabitants of the area, these emigrant families were not driven out over the historical continuum—*they were never there in the first place.*

Dafna Yee, director of the JWD website, also explains that since "the borders of the Palestine territory were never clearly defined, it is safe to assume that a great many, if not most, of the 'Palestinians' never set foot in any part of what is now Israel and have as flimsy a claim to that identity as Arafat did"—Arafat was born in Egypt. She might also have mentioned Edward Said, another self-proclaimed Palestinian, who did in fact set foot in what is now Israel—he was born in a Jewish hospital in Jerusalem where his parents calculated that the probability of a safe delivery was higher than in an Arab hospital, and was subsequently raised in Cairo where he spent the first twelve years of his life before moving to the West. With regard to Israel, fictions tend to multiply exponentially. In particular, that Israel was built on something called "Palestinian land" through a process of invasion and displacement is a myth that continues to gather momentum. On the contrary, Israel is not only the ancient Jewish homeland, but in modern times it was founded as a nation by legal land purchases and legitimized by the United Nations.

Undeterred, Palestinian human rights activists continue to propound a bald-faced lie. For example, Susan Abulhawa, author of the novel *The Scar of David*, asserted in an article for the Paris magazine *Libèration* (March 18, 2008) that Israel was established on "the ancient land of Palestine," a historical artifice created on the instant. The reader will look in vain in Abulhawa's piece for any mention of the fact that between 1932 and 1944 half a million Arabs poured *into* Palestine to profit from conditions prevailing in the Jewish communities. That she claims in the same article that "Jesus was Palestinian" may tell us something about the Palestinian style of argument. The Palestinian "narrative" is a synthetic athenaeum whose textual repertory is, for the most part, either forged or imagined. Palestinians fall back on what is by now a classic maneuver: the attempt to achieve unity and yeast up purpose by the denial of fact. But the fact is that the "Palestinian entity" *as such* is non-historic and would more accurately be defined as a *Palestinian nonentity*, its documentary grounding largely fabricated and its political aspirations dependent on a volatile mix of ignorance and deception.[7]

At the risk of belabouring the point, let me recapitulate succinctly to help us get a handle on the facts. The Israeli "occupation" is, to begin with, by no means an occupation in the accepted sense of an unwarranted invasion of a neighbouring country's territory, such as Hitler's occupying the Sudetenland and Czechoslovakia, or the United States annexing Texas, or, for that matter, Canada occupying Indian lands. On the contrary, it was the *result* of a premeditated attack upon Israel by the hostile surrounding nations, *which were intent upon occupying Israel.* Secondly, Israel no longer maintains a presence in southern Lebanon or Gaza, and a defensive slice of 6% of the West Bank, for which it is willing to swap an equivalent amount of Israeli territory, does not constitute an "occupation." Thirdly, "Palestine" as a country never existed but was always a part of some larger governing unit. And fourthly, a significant number of those who regard themselves as "Palestinian" are, in the greater historical purview, relative latecomers to the region, in this sense like many Jews who arrived in Israel in the various waves of immigration—but with this crucial difference, that the former had no ancestral roots in what is today called Israel, and many not even in the West Bank.

These are facts that have been suppressed, forgotten, distorted or turned inside out. In *How to Do things with Words*, Philosopher J.L. Austin has made a useful distinction between two kinds of speech acts, the referential and the constative. The referential delineates an actual state of affairs, the constative establishes not a quality but a social function. Austin offers an analogy from baseball: the ball may travel across the center of the plate, a perfect strike, but if the umpire calls "ball," that's how it registers on the scoreboard and operates in the game. For much of the world today, umpires (and crowds) engaged in the production of their own referents and bent on the reconstruction of reality, an Israeli "strike" will almost always count as a "ball." The referential has been reconfigured as the constative, despite what a later replay may bring to light—the Gaza beach hoax, the Lebanese ambulance hoax, the al-Durah hoax, the Mohammed Omer hoax, and so on. When it comes to Israel, the constative will almost always trump the referential and a collective assessment obliterate an objective factor. The Israeli pitcher throws a strike; the Arab batter receives a base on balls. An intimate congruence has been *performatively* created between the report and the referent minus the slightest hint of the semantic distance that stretches between the two. The former remains parasitic upon the latter.

Archeologist and historian David Meir-Levy makes this clear in his new book, with its Austinesque title *History Upside Down: The Roots of Palestinian Fascism and the Myth of Israeli Aggression*, in which he tries to dig up the buried facts and return to the referential. He points out that "the Arabs of the area had their own designation for the region: *Balad esh-Sham* (the country, or province of Damascus.)" It was only after the 1967 war that the PLO reframed the issue by "inventing a 'historic Palestine' *ex nihilo*, an ancient 'Palestinian people' who had lived in their 'homeland' from 'time immemorial' [and] who were forced from their homeland by the Zionists…" The idea of a Palestinian nation was hatched, principally by Yasser Arafat, "for political purposes and to justify and legitimize terrorism and genocide." Arafat himself did not disguise his intentions. In his own words, the aim of the PLO was "not to impose our will on [Israel], but to destroy it in order to take its place." Further, no Palestinian leader, neither Arafat nor Abbas nor any of their chief negotiators, have acknowledged that *there are no 1967 borders* to which Israel is required to return. In fact, there are only armistice lines, and the Jordanian peace agreement with Israel specified that these armistice lines would have no bearing on future negotiations to determine final borders. Lord Caradon himself, Britain's ambassador to the United Nations and one of the framers of Resolution 242, stated in the *Beirut Daily Star* for June 12, 1974, that "It would have been wrong to demand that Israel return to its positions of June 4, 1967, because those positions were undesirable and artificial."

In this context, it is obvious that the propaganda war against Israel, joined by many in the West, is an indispensable part of the violent campaign to erase the country from the map. The strategy at work in all these instances of malfeasance is obvious: if the lie about Israel is repeated often enough, it will eventually be accepted as truth. Strike three will be called as ball four. The effectiveness of this strategy is borne out by the findings of a BBC global survey, released in March 2007, which skewers Israel as the most negatively-viewed country in the world and shows how successful the BBC and the like-minded media have been in pursuing their hatchet job on the Jewish state. This clandestine design has penetrated into the domain of presumably objective scholarship as well. The prestigious *Macmillan Reference USA* encyclopedia contains an entry on antisemitism culled in part from a controversial article in the journal *Race Traitor*, authored by the anti-Zionist Jew Noel Ignatiev. The brunt of the article makes Jews themselves responsible for antisemitism, which brings the rationale for the creation of the Jewish state into question. Cognitive distortion is the name of the game. As Aldous Huxley has one of his characters reflect in *Brave New World*, suggesting the famous dicta of Hitler and Goebbels about the reiterative efficacy of the "Big Lie," "Sixty-two thousand four hundred repetitions make one truth. Idiots!"

There can be no doubt whatsoever, then, that the blanket attainting of Israel is only the passe-partout of the new antisemitism. Here Natan Sharansky gets it right. In *The Case for Democracy*, he lays it down that whereas "classical anti-Semitism is aimed at the Jewish people and the Jewish religion, the new anti-Semitism is aimed at the Jewish state. Since this anti-Semitism can hide behind the veneer of legitimate criticism, it is much more difficult to expose." The hitman is still firing away, only in this case he is using a silencer. Sharansky's 3-D test helps to sort out the fuzziness between antisemitism and anti-Israeli or anti-Zionist attitudes: Demonization (Israel as an outlaw country), Double-standards (when Israel is measured by a different yardstick from that applied to other nations and communities), and Delegitimization (undermining the very right of Israel to secure existence). When this test is administered, many if not most anti-Zionist and anti-Israeli arguments can be seen for what they are, antisemitic diatribes in mufti. Anti-Israelism is nothing less than the most fashionable form of antisemitism going. Even so unlikely a source as the U.S. State Department has admitted the fact; in a report issued on March 14, 2008, it described the high-decibel criticism of Israel in today's world as a new kind of antisemitism over and above traditional antisemitic acts.

Let us not waddle around the issue, as those who love to censure Israel under cover of a false impartiality are given to. *If it walks like a duck….* The peculiar gait of Barack Obama should give us pause. We should not be surprised that Obama awarded the prestigious Medal of Freedom to Mary Robinson who, as United Nations High Commissioner for Human Rights, presided over the infamous anti-Israel hatefest at the Durban I conference of racism. We know that Obama sat for twenty years beneath Pastor Jeremiah Wright's Jew-bashing pulpit. We recall that he was friendly with former PLO operative Rashid Khalidi whose oeuvre is devoted to delegitimizing the Jewish state. It is probably no accident that two of Obama's closest affiliates are Rahm Emanuel and David Axelrod, Jews who give every indication of regarding their own community with disfavor. Obama's much-touted "summit" of Jewish community leaders at the White House in July 2009 privileged groups critical of Israel like the Israel Policy Forum, Americans for Peace Now and the fringe J Street, but excluded conservative pro-Israel groups like the Zionist Organization of America, the Jewish Institute for National Security and the Lubavitcher movement. It is also curious, to say the least, that the American President has stated categorically that he does not wish to meddle in the affairs of other nations or dictate solutions to their internal problems, yet this has not prevented him interfering aggressively in Israeli affairs and imposing his prescription to resolve the so-called settlement controversy. One may be pardoned, perhaps, for suspecting a certain duplicity at work.

A prime example of this split dynamic—declaratively working for peace in the Middle East while effectively shilling for Israel's enemies—was provided by the actions of Spain's socialist Prime Minister, Jose Luis Rodriguez Zapatero, who seemed unaware that he was acting in a typical *zarzuela*, a Spanish satirical operetta, all his own. During a rally in Alicante in July 2006 protesting the Israeli response to Hizbullah's unprovoked attack on the country, Zapatero accused Israel of using "abusive force" and then posed for the camera wearing a keffiyeh. He later wafted another facsimile peace plan calling for renewed dialogue between Israel and the Palestinians, without addressing the issue of Palestinian recidivism which seeks to destroy the Jewish state whether by violence or the "right of return."

He took a different line, however, when it came to the Basque terrorist militias on Spanish soil—militias, incidentally, which do not consider themselves as terrorists but as "resistance fighters" struggling to acquire an independent homeland in what they regard as their rightful territory. After the ETA bombing of Madrid's Barajas International Airport in December 2006, Zapatero suspended talks with the separatist group. So much for "dialogue."[8]

Zapatero was equally outraged when the ETA exploded a bomb outside a military barracks in Legutiano on May 14, 2008, killing one guard and wounding another four; his Interior Minister described the event as a "horrific attack, which is especially evil for its indiscriminate nature" (*Helendipity Weblog*, May 15, 2008). The attack was no doubt horrific, indiscriminate and evil because it occurred in Spain and not in Israel where such atrocities are perfectly okay. After the two recent bombings in Burgos and Mallorca on July 28 and 30, 2009 respectively, wounding 60 people and killing two policemen, Zapatero denounced "these vile assassins" and vowed to bring them to justice (*France 24 International News*, August 1, 2009). There is no problem, it seems, with proper identification and punitive action when terrorist mayhem occurs close to home. It is obviously acceptable to apply double standards to a merely notional "outlaw country," aka Israel, which is by every international standard a legitimate nation whose right to secure existence is threatened, but terrorist irruptions in one's own country are another matter entirely. If this is not pure pharisaism and moral bad faith, then nothing is.

Recently, Zapatero's Spanish Agency for Industrial Development Cooperation, part of the Foreign Ministry, has been funding activists who visit Israel to rebuild Palestinian homes demolished, for military or legal reasons, by the Israeli government. At the same time, as Soeren Kern, a senior analyst for the *Grupo de Estudios Estratégicos* in Madrid, reports, Zapatero has "himself been on a demolition spree all across Spain…tearing down illegal homes built by Gypsies and Moroccans," along with hundreds of others. "Of course," Kern comments, "Spaniards would be outraged if the Israeli government dispatched activists to rebuild the six dwellings in the Madrid district of Las Mimbreras that were deemed illegal and torn down in July

2009. Or the dozens of illegal homes that have been torn down in the La Canada Real district of Madrid during the last two years. Or the homes of 236 families that were levelled in the El Salobral district of Madrid in December 2007 in order to build an industrial area" (*Pajamas Media*, August 15, 2009).

The question of double standards came to the fore once again with respect to the Free Gaza Movement whose boats ran the Israeli naval blockade of Gaza in August 2008 with a cargo of hearing aids. Sponsored by such tainted bodies as the International Solidarity Movement, the Palestinian Center for Human Rights, the Israel Committee Against House Demolitions, among others—all of them extreme groups endorsed by Hamas—the Movement's first small but well-financed flotilla left Gaza for Cyprus with seven Palestinians aboard the *SS Free Gaza* and the *SS Liberty*. There was not a word in their various communiqués about 23-year-old Israeli soldier, Gilad Shalit, kidnapped on Israeli territory by Hamas in June 2006 and held in illegal detention since that time. There was no attempt to arrange for visits from the International Red Cross, as sanctioned by international law which has been pointedly ignored by Hamas. There was no offer to broker his release and to include him among the Palestinians given free passage on their vessels.

When it comes to the call of human rights, the members of the Free Gaza Movement might have availed themselves of the hearing aids they so generously donated to their hosts. Or alternatively, they might have donated these amplifying devices to the international community, which is severely hearing-impaired, rather than to Hamas, whose ears prick up at the faintest whisper of complicity with the human rights of the Jewish state.

8

A House Divided

We should not deceive ourselves into believing, were the struggle in the Middle East to be resolved one day, that a slippered amity would descend upon the region and that the terrorist internationale would somehow be defanged and gentled. Neither Judaism nor Israel is the question here. As has been noted by Israeli scientist Haim Harari, author of *A View from the Eye of the Storm: Terror and Reason in the Middle East*, Israel is not the central issue but an opportune pretext. The atrocities perpetrated by Islamic culture are largely *sui generis*. "The millions who died in the Iran-Iraq war had nothing to do with Israel. The mass murder happening right now in Sudan...has nothing to do with Israel. [The Algerian massacres] have nothing to do with Israel. Saddam Hussein did not invade Kuwait, endanger Saudi Arabia and butcher his own people because of Israel. Egypt did not use poison gas against Yemen in the 60s because of Israel. Assad the Father did not kill tens of thousands of his own citizens in one week in El Hamma in Syria because of Israel. The Taliban control of Afghanistan and the civil war there had nothing to do with Israel. The Libyan blowing up of the Pan-Am flight had nothing to do with Israel..." Nor did the Paris metro bombing of 1995, the suicide crash of EgyptAir 990 with its 217 victims, the Beslan schoolhouse slaughter, the British terrorist plots and transport bombings have anything to do with Israel. Nor, we might add, do the train bombings and street carnage carried out by Islamic radicals in India or the Sunni car bombings and streetlamp hangings or the raids and ambushes of Moqtada Sadr's Shi'ite army in Iraq or the Syrian-backed state murders in Lebanon or the knacker's yard that is Pakistan or the unspeakable atrocities perpetrated in Gaza by Fatah and Hamas or the sporadic bloodbaths in the Philippines or the violence in southern Thailand have anything to do with Israel.

Presumptive Arab "moderates" and their Western partners continue to insist that if the Israeli/Palestinian problem were to be settled, the conflict between the Islamic world and the West would be resolved and the belligerents reconciled. This pious hope, unfortunately, which is a mainstay of Western policy and a key plank in President Obama's rather wooden Middle East initiative, is pure eyewash. For as Harari has noted, the Israeli/Palestinian dispute is nothing less than one of the current pretexts enlisted by the Islamic world to expedite its campaign against Israeli and Western interests and security. One can be entirely confident that, were Israel to be defeated or agree to terms that would deprive it of territorial and political viability, Muslim animosity and terrorist activities would not simply dissipate; they would assert themselves ever more vigorously.

"The borders of Islam are bloody," remarked Samuel Huntington in *The Clash of Civilizations*, and so are its outposts. Those who wish to get at the "root" of Islamic bloodlust should read their way back into Islamic history and thought, starting with the apostles of jihadist violence Sayyid Qutb and Maulana Maudoodi, proceeding to their source in the medieval religious thinker Ibn Taymiyyah who called for holy war, and come to rest finally in *his* source, the Koran. Surrendering Israel as an oblation to its enemies would not make an iota of difference. And we in the liberal West are only abetting such depravity in refusing to speak out against the barbarism of its agents, cowering in fear at the possibility of reprisal or even justifying what is nothing less than the debauchery of evil. We can see ourselves in the mirror of Psalm 22, if we only look: "The wicked walk on every side, when the vilest men are exalted."

But all this does not imply that the Jew is a pristinely innocent being. The history of Judaism reads like a tape-measure scroll of strife, estrangement and rupture, from the time of the splitting of the nation into two warring kingdoms and the early Temple magnates glorying in their perquisites at the expense of the common people, through the centuries of religious factionalism and reciprocal excommunication, the profound antipathy between assimilated Jews and their irredentist counterparts in Jerusalem, Tiberias, Safed and Hebron as well as the Caste-like contempt of Western Jewish intellectuals for the *Ostjuden*, that is, their plebeian and "uneducated" East European brethren, the shame of the Jewish Councils in Nazi Europe collaborating with their murderers, to the present moment in the newly restored nation where left-wing peace activists and "post-Zionist" intellectuals strive to erode the Jewish character of the state and so deprive it of its legitimacy. The Israeli Left, dancing around the golden calf of a factitious peace, represents the gravest danger to the survival of the country; in the words of Israeli literary critic Gershon Shaked, they have "subverted the Zionist metaplot," that is, pulled the rug out from under the very notion of Israel's *raison d'être* while chasing a corposant of fire and ash. At the same time, the ultra-Orthodox (*Agudat Israel*) seek to establish a *de facto* theocratic protectorate under God, and so deprive the Jewish state of its social and democratic foundation as a modern nation.

Indeed, secular post-Zionists of the Left and religious anti-Zionists on the Right have much in common in their revulsion for the state of Israel, many of their respective members sharing the belief, formulated in the Satmar Hasidic movement's Grand Rebbe Joel Teitelbaum's 1958 book *VaYoel Moshe*, that "It is because of the Zionists that six million Jews were killed." From this warped optic, it is Zionism itself that is mainly responsible for antisemitism around the world, as if two millennia of persecution had never happened and the vicious pogroms predating the Zionist movement were a figment of the Jewish imagination, as if the misnamed "Jewish problem" had not long pre-existed Zionist activism and might not be better regarded as its cause rather than its consequence. For the anti-Zionists, the state of Israel is a violation of Jewish teachings; for the post-Zionists, the state of Israel is a historical mistake, which is why they wish to repeal the Jewish Law of Return, one of the central platforms in the founding of the country as a sanctuary for homeless, dispossessed and immigrant Jews the world over. That, under the circumstances they propose, both anti-Zionists and post-Zionists would cease to exist at the hands of their enemies does not seem to have occurred to these nominal disputants—or perhaps it has, which is even more perturbing. That the same fate would befall those of their countrymen and co-religionists who think otherwise also appears to be a matter of little importance to them.

Altogether, such lack of collegiality, amounting to a clash of intrinsically insoluble paradoxes, is the shadow side of Jewish life which must be frankly admitted in the interests of both honesty and self-understanding. Across the centuries and today in Israel, it is as if we are watching a repeat of the biblical combat between siblings, between Cain and Abel, Jacob and Esau, Joseph and his brothers, and we are moved to ask: will it ever end?[9] And in the context of the ongoing fray between the secular state and the Rabbinate-backed outposters, it is as if we are seeing a lesser version of the battle between the armies of Joab and Abner or the dynastic violence between the pro-Hellenists and the Hasmoneans, but one nevertheless presaging the possibility of civil unrest. It is almost as if there must be something in the collective psyche of the *Yishuv*, the body of the Jewish people in the Holy Land, that breeds *sinat chinam*, baseless hatred, among themselves. It is almost as if there is an insatiable death wish eating away at the Jewish soul.

And this is not to mention the jam-packed stadium of mainly left-wing Diasporite Jews who have turned against their own, who vilify and seek to delegitimize the Jewish state and Jewish peoplehood. A group of celebrity British Jews have embraced the opportunity presented by the times and formed a new movement called the IJV (Independent Jewish Voices) which, according to the acerbic, anti-Israeli newspaper the *Independent*, is intended to create a platform for dissent without its signatories "being accused of disloyalty or being dismissed as self-hating." Its members include such well-known leftist Israel-bashers as Harold Pinter, Mike Leigh, Jaqueline Rose and Eric Hobsbawm, who have never participated in Jewish life and have no connection to Jewish community and worship, which bodes poorly for balanced commentary and informed criticism. The IJV's first act was to publish an open letter in the *Times* and *Guardian*, also noted anti-Israeli dailies, attacking the Jewish establishment in England for its loyalty to Israel and its presumed neglect of Palestinian human rights, but without so much as mentioning the treaty violations, aid embezzlement, propaganda exaggerations, continued incitement and murder campaigns sanctioned by the Palestinian Authority and the Hamas government. This missive was in many ways only a reprise of another vicious and wrong-headed letter printed in *The Guardian* in

December 2006, in which British writer John Berger, film director Ken Loach, novelist Arundhati Roy, and ninety-five other signatories proceeded to dump on Israel, also quoting the anti-Israel remarks of Archbishop Desmond Tutu.

Little better is the Institute for Jewish Policy Research think tank, the only one of its kind in the U.K., whose director, Antony Lerman, taking a page from Judah Magnes' discredited, pre-1948 Brit Shalom movement, supports the supplanting of Israel by a bi-national state with an Arab majority. An outfit called Jews for Justice for Palestinians (JFJP) sponsored a press advertisement blaming Israel for its incursion into Gaza after the Hamas kidnapping of Israeli soldier Gilad Shalit. A new Jewish group, an offshoot of the JFJP, has emerged to promote the boycott of Israeli goods—its leader, Deborah Fink, declares that Israel should not be called the Jewish state but the Satanic state. Plainly in agreement with Fink, a group of 100 Jewish anti-Zionists, including the aforementioned Pinter, refused to celebrate Israel's 60th anniversary, publishing a letter in *The Guardian* decrying the foundation of the state and accusing Israel of every imaginable (and imaginary) crime while editing out any reference to Palestinian terrorism and malfeasance and sailing right over the tortuous histology of the region. The letter accuses Israel of being "founded on terrorism, massacres and the dispossession of another people from their land," of being a country that "violates international law, that is inflicting a monstrous collective punishment on the civilian population of Gaza and that continues to deny to Palestinians their human rights and national aspirations." Had the signatories turned their oratory on the history of Arab conquest over a millennium and a half, the practice of the Sudanese government, the atrocious human rights records of Alawite Syria, Ba'athist Iraq and Khomeinite Iran, the theocratically-driven savagery of Hamas and Hizbullah, the Russian levelling of Chechnya or the Chinese invasion and despoliation of Tibet, such fiery words would have made good sense. In the present context, the letter is nothing but an instance of ignorant and vitriolic bluster, a selective and reductionist reading of the historical register to accord with an unvindicable *parti pris*.

No less disturbing is the psychological clustering of the vast majority of American Jews who support the Democratic party (like their counterparts in Canada who vote Liberal), which is increasingly inimical to Israel and, ultimately, to Jewish concerns. This is a phenomenon I am tempted to call "overboarding," a psychic consensus founded on a kind of mass hypnosis that does not take actual conditions into account. Then we have the RHR-NA (Rabbis for Human Rights North America) which supports the New York based CCR (Center for Constitutional Rights)—the CCR has sued several high Israeli security officials for "war crimes," although neither the CCR nor the good rabbis have filed lawsuits against known Palestinian war criminals. To add injury to injury, the New Israel Fund and the Jewish Agency provide funding to the Mossawa Center, an Arab-Israeli apparatus, which opposes the Jewish Law of Return and supports the Palestinian "right of return," the redesign of the national flag, the elevating of Arabic to the status of Mother Tongue and the creation of a bi-national state. The NIF has also funded Arab groups like Adalah and the intellectuals and political activists behind the Haifa Declaration, published on May 21, 2007, which would completely eviscerate Israel's character as the Jewish national home.

And how condone the UPZ (Union of Progressive Zionists) which regularly imports extreme left-wing Israelis to American college campuses in an effort to popularize anti-Zionist sentiment, castigating Israeli measures for self-defense against Palestinian terrorists as illegitimate and immoral? Or the United Jewish Communities which in October 1999 had planned to award Yasser Arafat the Isaiah Peace Prize, backing down only after its intention was leaked to the press and now maintaining that the affair had been misreported? Or groups like the Committee on New Alternatives in the Middle East (CONAME) and the former Diaspora-Israel Relations organization known as Breira (Hebrew for "alternative" or "choice") which opposed U.S. military aid to Israel during the Yom Kippur war. Or the Israel Policy Forum which objects to American politicians who express sympathy with Israel and who entertain doubts about Palestinian sincerity—the IPF's director, M.J. Rosenberg, accuses Jews living in their ancient city of Hebron as a provocational minority which "routinely abuses the majority Palestinians," urges the U.S. to cease “pandering” to Israel and regards Tel Aviv, where “gay Palestinians come…to be part of the lively gay scene” as “the embodiment of the Zionist dream”? It seems not to have occurred to this Jewish sage that Zionism is not about sleeping in the arms of members of the same sex but about sleeping in the assurance that one will awaken in the morning.

Reconstructionist rabbi and founder of *Tikkun* magazine Michael Lerner is equally suspect. True to his Berkeley campus roots, Lerner fires adjectives like “repressive” and “fascistic” at the Jewish state, accepts Palestinian violence for which he blames Israeli practices and policies, and accuses Israel “for not having fulfilled the terms of the Oslo Accord”—all instances of the inside-out argumentation favoured by the *apikorosim*, the “wicked sons” of Jewish public life. Like most of the world’s news outlets, Lerner never mentions that the Oslo Declaration of Principles *was never ratified* by the PLO, nor that Article 19 of the PLO Covenant rejects the 1947 UN partition of Palestine and that Article 20 denies the Jewish historical relationship to the Holy Land. The World Jewish Congress is no better, having objected to the publishing of the Mohammed cartoons in a Danish newspaper as an affront to Muslim sensitivities and patronized the venomously antisemitic Louis Farrakhan who heads the Black Muslim movement in the U.S. More recently, the WJC embraced one of the most vicious Presidential antisemites outside the Arab world, Venezuela’s Hugo Chavez, for restoring diplomatic ties with Israel, forgetting that 25% of Venezuela’s embattled Jewish population have emigrated under his watch, that Chavez pursues close relations with Holocaust deniers such as Iran’s Ahmadinejad and, according to recent reports, is supplying Iran with uranium for its nuclear program.

Not to be outdone, the Union of Reform Judaism has established a friendly relation and organizational bond with the Islamic Society of North America which has demonstrable ties with several radical Muslim groups and has been named in a federal trial concerning fundraising for Hamas as an unindicted co-conspirator; the URJ also objected to the Congress “passing one-sided pro-Israeli resolutions” and its president, Rabbi Eric Yoffie, while cooperating with the Islamic Society of North America, has refused to work with Christian

Zionists who support the Jewish state. The American Jewish Committee sent a letter to Secretary of State Hilary Clinton urging her not to boycott an upcoming anti-Jewish hatefest. Fortunately they were unsuccessful. And what to make of the Spertus Institute of Jewish Studies in Chicago mounting an exhibit, entitled "Imaginary Coordinates," displaying maps and postcards designed to foreground the Palestinian narrative? Its president, Howard Sulkin, defended the anti-Israel spin of the exposition by falling back on the usual opiate of "inspir[ing] dialogue on the critical issues of our time" (*Chicago Tribune*, June 20, 2008). To the contrary, a creeping dhimmitude is spreading like a stain in the Jewish community.

One can only be appalled at the spectacle of secular Jewish and Israeli students as well as visiting Israeli professors, clearly members of the radical Left, seen applauding Ahmadinejad during his talk at Columbia University, undeterred by the fact that his stated intent is to wipe them off the face of the earth. That so many American Jews—78% according to recent polls—were, behind the Presidential campaign of Barack Obama, whose friends and advisors included intensively anti-Israel figures like Zbigniew Brzezinski (who in a recent interview suggested that American fighter jets engage Israeli warplanes should Israel attack Iran), Susan Rice, Merrill McPeak, Brent Scowcroft, Samantha Power, Robert Malley, Anthony Lake, Rashid Khalidi, pro-Palestinian activist Ali Abunimah (the founder of the *The Electronic Intifada* website), and the antisemitic Jeremiah Wright Jr., pastor of the Trinity United Community Church, is an equally mournful sight. (Wright has called Jews "bloodsuckers" and is, as well, as a friend of Farrakhan.)

When over 300 American rabbis formed a support group for Obama, "you know something is going on," as the group's website, *rabbisforobama.com*, declares—which is to say, that something desperately wrong with the Jewish community is indeed going on. Approximately half of this passel of rabbis are members of the *Brit Tzedek V'Shalom*, or Jewish Alliance for Justice and Peace, an extremist left wing group that encourages the Palestinians, opposes Israeli action against Hamas and has good things to say about the International Solidarity Movement. More recently a group of

American rabbis initiated something they call *Ta'anit Tzedek*, or the Jewish Fast for Gaza, as if the Gazans were not responsible for the last round of hostilities and as if there were no hungry people in Israel.

Adding to the rota of these "friends of Israel," a new "progressive" Jewish organization has now appeared on the American scene, calling itself J Street. Ostensibly committed to "moderation" and "balance," it is merely another far-Left, Jewish anti-Israel political action committee like the British IJV, rejecting the cooperation of the Christian Zionist movement which is one of the few real friends Israel has among the Churches, pressing for direct talks with Hamas and Iran and supported by prominent figures like Ron Pudnak, Avraham Burg and David Kimche who have worked in various ways to damage Israel's interests and credibility while embracing the Palestinians as trusted partners for peace. Its Advisory Council also boasts several magian names, such as former Obama advisor Robert Malley, who resigned when his outreach to Hamas came to light, Daniel Levy formerly of the Israeli PMO and Rabbi Toba Spitzer, President of the Reconstructionist Rabbinical Association, who feature among a multiple minyan of holy men. Jimmy Carter is one of their heroes—as he is of another organization, Jewish Voice for Peace, which presented the former President with a letter approving of his overtures to Hamas in April 2008. "Jimmy Carter speaks for me," the letter avows. Indeed he does.

Canada too has its delicate sufficiency of tergiversating Jews and *shtadlan*s, or Court Jews and panderers. For example, we can field the Alliance of Concerned Jewish Canadians who object to the "occupation and siege of the Palestinian territories," once again revealing an utter lack of knowledge and understanding of the historical context as well as of the present reality. The ACJC had no objection to the vile antisemitic belchings of Durban I, praising it instead for highlighting the plight of the Palestinians, urged Canadian participation in Durban II, and regards Israel as a "blatantly discriminatory" state. No less contemptibly, the Shalom-Salaam "dialogue group" plays fast and loose with the facts in inveighing against Israeli "aggression" and supposed brutality. Our Reconstructionist synagogues are racing down the same accommodationist path, sponsoring debates and colloquia weighted toward the Palestinian cause in the interests of "openness" and "fairness" and thus subtly contributing to the growing international misperception that Israel is closed and unfair. The Canadian Council for Israel and Jewish Advocacy (CIJA) has vetted an internal document titled "The 10 Commandments" instructing its members to take a low public profile. Commandment 5 states, in part: "Do not directly attack or assign blame to the Palestinians or their leadership." Commandment 7: "Do not ask the government of Canada to appear—or be—more favourable to Israel." Commandment 9: "Do not attack the media for being biased against Israel." This form of anti-advocacy is known by the Yiddish expression as the *sha shtil* philosophy—hush hush, do not speak up—as practised during the Shoah to stunning counter-effect.

Recently I came across a letter to the editor in my city newspaper, the *Montreal Gazette*, signed by a group of "young Jews." They wrote mainly in support of the Palestinian cause, proclaiming their opposition to "the immoral and impractical policies that deny Palestinians equal rights," calling for "an end to the siege on Gaza" and for "a permanent ceasefire," putting the onus on Israel for "genuine peace negotiations that end the Israeli occupation of Gaza, the West Bank, and East Jerusalem, dismantle the annexation barrier and the illegal settlements, implement the UN resolutions recognizing the rights of Palestinians," and so on. They have probably never heard of Eugene Rostow, one of the leading architects of UN Resolution 242, who explained that the Resolution "allows Israel to administer the territories it occupied in 1967 until 'a just and lasting peace in the Middle East' is achieved" and that "the Jews have the same right to settle there as they have to settle in Haifa" (*The New Republic*, October 21, 1991). The children conclude by stating that they can no longer "justify a system of oppression that promises continual destruction for Israelis and Palestinians alike."

At this point in the development of my argument, it should be utterly clear that these young Samaritans, like so many of their ilk here and elsewhere in the world, are wrong or misinformed on pretty well every count. These are kids who do not know what it is to be persecuted, who grew up in safety and comfort in a tolerant and advanced society at a time when antisemitism was at its lowest ebb, and who, not being Israeli, have never had to dodge bullets, defuse bombs, take cover in shelters or worry about suicide bombers suddenly manifesting in a Second Cup or in their university libraries. It is such fortunate ignorance that permits them to spout their noble and "enlightened" sentiments about highly dubious UN resolutions (engineered by an Arab and Muslim-influenced majority), the security fence (which has reduced the incidence of terror attacks on Israeli soil), an "occupation" which is nothing of the sort, imputed Palestinian innocence and trumpeted Israeli wrongdoing. It is such bland and unruffled self-satisfaction which has spared them the drudgery of having to disinter the historical facts hidden under the sediment of popular opinion—a sediment built up layer by layer by every shovelful of such confusion, misinformation and self-exaltation. Their letter is titled "Criticism is not disloyalty." This is very true, but it is equally true that factual illiteracy is not criticism. And that the easy compassion of the uninitiated is neither rigorous insight nor educated feeling.

"The philistine Jew is part of what's wrong with the world, a modality of its sickness," wrote Canada's greatest poet, Irving Layton, in the Foreword to *The Swinging Flesh*; the Jew's place, rather, is "beside the Jewish visionaries, scholars, poets, and rebels." Layton would have been horrified at the spectacle of so many "good Jews" siding with Goliath, earning them twice over the epithet of "philistine." All this suggests what may well be the major question for contemporary Judaism: Can Jews survive themselves? One may well wonder if the curse of David may yet come to pass: "Let their table be made a snare, and a trap, and a stumbling block, and a recompence unto them: Let their eyes be darkened, that they may not see, and bow down their back alway" (*Romans* 11: 9, 10).

It gets even worse. Such specimens of apostasy pale in comparison with the activities of Jewish historians such as Ariel Toaff and Sergio Luzzatto. According to the published comments of those who have pre-read the book, Toaff's latest offering, *Bloody Passover: The Jews of Europe and Ritual Murders*, has revived the ancient blood libel, appearing to suggest that there might have been some truth to the accusations that the Italian Jews of Trent committed acts of ritual murder in 1475 in order to make their passover *matzot* with the blood of Christian children. Toaff afterward publicly claimed that he does not credit these accusations and halted distribution of the book in order to "re-edit" the offending passages. At the same time, in an interview he gave to the Israeli daily *Haaretz*, he reiterated that "within Ashkenazi Judaism there were extremist groups that could have committed such acts." The operative term is "could have"—but an "anything is possible" argument in such a sensitive and explosive context is a violation of both personal propriety and historical probity. In a subsequent spread in the *Jerusalem Post*, Toaff promised to clarify the issue and to "state that the Jews did not *routinely* murder Christian children for their blood" (italics mine). Whatever Toaff actually believes, he should have known that *Bloody Passover* would stoke the oven of antisemitism. Luzzatto, for his part, praised the book in the *Corriere della Sera*, stating that "A minority of fundamentalist Ashkenazis…carried out human sacrifice." Luzzatto seems to have forgotten that in Jewish *kashrut* or dietary laws, observed by all Orthodox communicants, blood is *tref*, "unfit to eat." Toaff asserts that the rabbis permitted the use of dried blood for curative purposes and that "There was always the possibility that some crazy person would do something." Again, a "possibility" is not a fact, and its insertion into a combustible situation can only be destructive.

Toaff has declared that he is willing to be crucified for the truth. This is certainly a noble sentiment, but when a historian relies on tall tales, calumnies or even historical aberrations on which to build a thesis stigmatizing a people or, in effect, provides scaffolding *in whatever way* to shaky structures of malign implication, we are perilously close to something that is not the truth. We are, in fact, perilously close to innuendo and contumely. In the contemporary context of resurgent antisemitism around the world, all Jews are tarred by extrapolation—even if, in the case of the blood libel, the only blood known to have flowed was Jewish blood. Toaff seems to have forgotten the accusations of ritual murder that fueled the European outbreak of antisemitism toward the end of the 19th century and carried over into the 20th. One must ask whether he really believes this could not happen again and that his "research" might not be a contributing factor.[10] The blood libel is a standard motif in the Muslim world and is now leaking into the West as well, as witness a double truck feature in Sweden's largest daily, *Aftonbladet*, for August 18, 2009, accusing the Israeli army of harvesting the organs of abducted Palestinians.

Yet another scandal that erupted at the same time as the Toaff controversy, involving Israeli filmmaker Ran Edelist who directed a documentary entitled *Ruach Shaked* about an Israeli reconnaissance unit operating in the Sinai during the Six Day War. The film purportedly claims that the unit had killed 250 Egyptian prisoners of war, a revelation which caused a media firestorm and led to members of the Egyptian parliament calling for the expulsion of the Israeli ambassador and the suspension of diplomatic relations with Israel. Edelist has admitted that errors were made with regard to voice over commentary and wrongly juxtaposed archival footage—in point of fact, the enemy casualties were actually Palestinian fedayeen trying to infiltrate into Israel and no POWs were executed. Such films, however, are pre-screened and it is hard to believe that such obtrusive blunders were overlooked, yet Edelist and Ittay Landsburg Nevo, head of the left-leaning Israel Broadcasting Authority, defended the production whose effect on the political scene could have been predicted with even the most rudimentary foresight.

Similarly, Israel's cable TV Channel 8 and the Jerusalem Cinematheque have been willing to fund anti-Zionist filmmaker Eyal Sivan, a typical self-abnegating Jew who managed to avoid his military service, was a speaker at "Israeli Apartheid Week" in London in 2007, and signed a public document condemning "the brutality and cruelty of Israeli policy" during the summer 2006 war with Hizbullah. Israel's Channel 2's Keshet franchise has frequently aired the docudramas of Motti Lerner, who plays fast and loose with the historical truth and believes, according to a paper he delivered at Brandeis University, that Israeli society is diseased, suffering from an "inability…to empathize with the Palestinians." Along the same lines, Shimon Dotan's documentary, *Hot House*, funded largely by Israel's New Foundation for Film and Television, sympathetically profiles female terrorist Ahlam Tamini who murdered fifteen people, eight of them children, in the bombing of the Sbarro pizzeria on August 9,

2001. Speaking for the Palestinians, whether terrorists, prisoners or civilians, Dotan comments: "We owe them empathy." More to the point, however, Frimet Roth, the mother of one of Tamini's young victims, writes in *Haaretz* (August 7, 2007): "Dotan is not alone in his conviction that to defend yourself against murderers is no different than murder. Many Israelis espouse and express this perverted morality."

As Isaiah prophesied, "thy destroyers and those that made thee waste shall go forth of thee."

9

And the Beat Goes On

Anti-Zionist and self-hating Jews, whether in the Holy Land or the Diaspora, feel that their best defense is to distance themselves from their faith, heritage and history, to disavow the Jewish state, or to displace their traditional preoccupation with justice and freedom onto other peoples and nations, speaking out not for Israel but for Darfur, Iraq and Palestine—as if so high-minded a gesture would parry the thrust of the fervent antisemite. Thus Tel Aviv writer Susan Nathan engages in an act of "revolutionary tourism" and moves into the Arab village of Tamra in northern Israel where, as she complains in *The Other Side of Israel: My Journey Across the Jewish/Arab Divide*, Israel "enforces a system of land apartheid," one of whose effects is that furniture is delivered late. Interestingly, she did not travel to Egypt or Syria to compare treatment of ordinary Arab citizens in those countries with those of Israel or move to a southern Israeli village like Sderot where she might have come under daily rocket attack. Similarly, columnist Larry Derfner, the *Jerusalem Post*'s resident Leftie, is more concerned with the plight of African refugees streaming into Israel, for whom he urges better treatment, than he is with the shell-shocked people of Sderot, for whom he recommends monetary compensation.

But it gets even more surreal than that. Hebrew University invites the two noted bigots and professional liars Stephen Walt and John Mearsheimer to lecture on the supposed intrigues of the "Israel Lobby." And at the same university, Sociology professor Eyal Ben-Ari and Education lecturer Edna Lomsky-Feder supervise a doctoral thesis by a certain Tal Nitzan, slated for publication by the University's Shaine Center for Research in Social Sciences, which claims that the absence of military rape of Palestinian women is no different from military rape itself, since it "strengthens the ethnic boundaries…just as military rape would have done"—Palestinian women are obviously humiliated and relegated to inferior status in being so loftily shunned by Israeli soldiers. If, that is, they are not already so dehumanized that, as the researcher explains, "consequently, a sexual act cannot be carried out with someone that is perceived as less than human." (Professor Ben-Ari, who sponsored the "Non-rape is racism" thesis, has now been arrested for suspected rape and sexual abuse of his students, who have accused him of conditioning good grades and research grants on their willingness to provide him with sexual favours. In one particularly succulent item, Ben-Ari billed the Shaine Center for a vibrator purchased for one of his students.)

Such acts of displacement and vilipendency are becoming increasingly popular among both Diaspora Jews and Israelis. Taking a page out of Derfner, Israeli students and members of the Knesset sign petitions on behalf of Sudanese refugees but are silent on the suffering of the residents of Sderot. These are Jews who have forgotten that the essence of Zionism, as Daniel Gordis explains in an article, "The Shame of It All," written for the Canadian Institute for Jewish Research, is "about changing the condition of the Jew, by changing the nature of the Jew." Instead, Jews and Israelis have once again "come to accept their victimization as part of nature. They are no longer shocked by what is done to them, no longer infuriated by their own powerlessness." Gordis refers appropriately to the celebrated poem by the Israeli Laureate, Chaim Nachman Bialik, entitled "The City of Slaughter," dealing with the infamous 1903 pogrom in Kishinev, capital of the Russian province of Bessarabia, in which Jewish men crouched in their cellars while their women were being beaten and raped. Kishinev, Gordis argues, has morphed into Sderot, with Jews sitting back, weak, defenseless and afraid, while their people are terrorized and killed. I cite a brief passage from the Bialik poem, one of the few which Gordis has not quoted, which seems to apply with particular relevance to the current situation: *the heirs/Of Hasmoneans lay with trembling knees,/Concealed and cowering—the sons of the Maccabees!/ ...crammed by scores in all the sanctuaries of their shame.*

These are Jews who, like the members of the left-wing peace movement *B'Tselem*, do everything in their power to prevent the

Israeli government from responding effectively to Palestinian attacks upon its civilian population, arguing that causing Palestinian civilian suffering constitutes a war crime. These are Jews who join the far left *Yesh Gvul* group and initiate legal proceedings against their own military. These are Jews like former foreign minister Shlomo Ben-Ami, now Vice-President of TICpax (the Toledo International Center for Peace), who in his last book *Scars of War, Wounds of Peace: The Israeli-Arab Tragedy*, speaks in defiance of both context and truth of a "ruthless Israeli army" perpetrating "atrocities and massacres…against the civilian Arab community." Or renowned orchestra conductor Daniel Barenboim, friend and collaborator of noted Israel-basher Edward Said, who accepts honorary PA "citizenship," saying that "the occupation has to stop," seemingly oblivious to the ambiguity of the term "occupation" and the cost in Israeli security and lives should the checkpoints and security fence be dismantled. Or celebrated author Amos Oz who, in the wake of several suicide bombings, writes an op-ed piece for *The New York Times* (April 11, 1995) linking Hamas and the Israeli conservative party Likud as mutually responsible for the carnage. Or his friend and equally renowned colleague Abraham Yehoshua who publishes an op-ed piece in Italy's *La Stampa* (January 20, 2008) calling on the US to withdraw its ambassador from Tel Aviv and deploring the power of the "Jewish Lobby." Or former member of the Knesset Uri Avnery who, in his memoir *1948*, in the part entitled "The Other Side of the Coin," puts these words into the mouth of a dead friend: "But what have you achieved? The state you dreamed of in the trenches is dead, even before it was born." Or Bard College professor Joel Kovel who has published a book called *Overcoming Zionism* in which he condemns the creation of Israel, places the term Islamo-Fascism in scare quotes, traffics in barefaced lies ("Israel's bombing of ambulances," its deliberate targeting of "humanitarian aid workers and UN observers," its causing of ecological disasters, etc.), and opts for the one-state solution beloved of closet antisemites. "What is wrong with the Jewish state," Kovel writes, "is the fact of being a Jewish state."

Of course, there is no mention of the diverse Muslim states which define themselves as precisely what they are, Muslim states (the Islamic Republic of Iran, the Islamic Republic of Pakistan, etc.) or of those countries in which Protestantism, Catholicism, Buddhism and the Orthodox Church are accepted as the national religions. If we are referring to the concept of "peoplehood," as in the "Jewish people," as a spurious foundation for the creation of a state, what are we then to make of the Syrian Arab Republic, the Arab Republic of Egypt, etc.? As for those Muslims like the aforementioned Saeb Erekat, and more recently Mahmoud Abbas, who object to the religious foundation of the Jewish state, it should be pointed out that Chapter 1, Article 2 of the Egyptian Constitution explicitly declares that "Islam is the State religion," both Egypt and Syria require that the President be a Muslim, and the *Palestinian Authority itself* stipulates in Article 5 of its Constitution that Islam is the "official Palestinian religion." Emmanuel Sivan in *Radical Islam* adds a new twist to the issue when, citing from sundry Arabic documents (e.g., *Nazarat Mu' asira fi Turathina* and *Wa-bi-l-Haqq*), he writes that the "New Radicals, like many of the older generation," entertained "a grudging respect toward Israel, held as an edifying example of a state built upon religion."

Such reflections do not register with those whom Andrew Silow-Carroll, editor in chief of the *New Jersey Jewish News*, calls the New Ontologists—those like the aforementioned Tony Judt, who is a major cog in the anti-Israel propaganda turbine. Or UCLA professor and author of *The Ottoman Tragedy* Gabriel Piterberg, another stalwart disciple of Edward Said, who sees the founding of Israel as an act of "ethnic cleansing" that can be repaired only by the creation of a single bi-national state minus its Jewish character. Or Gary Sussman, appointed vice president for external relations at Tel Aviv University, who compares Israel to apartheid South Africa, attacks the security fence, calls the terror-supporting Palestinians "plucky," and recommends "ending the occupation" in order to "empower Palestinian democrats," without specifying a single Palestinian democrat by name (*Jewish Quarterly*, Winter 2005/6). Or Richard Falk, Emeritus Professor of International Law and Practice at Princeton University and a yeoman supporter of Jimmy Carter, who has been appointed to succeed the anti-Israeli John Dugard as UN Special Rapporteur on the Palestinian Territories. Falk accuses Israel of subjecting Gaza to "life-endangering conditions of utmost cruelty," describes Palestinian rocket attacks on Israel as " rather pathetic strikes mainly taking place in response to Israeli violent provocations," and compares Israeli actions in the Territories to the Nazis' "collective atrocity" (*CounterCurrents.org*, July 7, 2007). Or Avraham Burg, ex-speaker of the Knesset and former Chair of the Jewish Agency, who in his newly released book, *Defeating Hitler*, and related interviews has repudiated Zionism as a philosophy of "human callousness," justifies suicide bombing as a legitimate response to Israeli "injustice and moral corruption," and compares Israel to Nazi Germany. I would guess that Burg has turned his gaze away from the spectacle of Hamas fighters on parade, emulating the goose-step and the straight-arm salute. He might have remembered what Saul Bellow wrote in 1975, that comparing "what the Nazis had done to the Jews resembled what Zionism had done to the Arabs [is] a parallel that no sane person would agree to."

Then there is political scientist Neve Gordon of Ben-Gurion University, a supporter of Norman Finkelstein and neoNazi Holocaust denier Ernst Zundel, and a contributor to such antisemitic websites as *Counterpunch*. Gordon is famous for describing the country that pays his salary, which he is apparently in no hurry to forgo, as an "apartheid state," and for having raised his arms in solidarity with Yasser Arafat in his Mukataa compound. Gordon's partner in infamy Moshe Machover, professor emeritus of King's College in London and a die-hard communist, is one of the worst of the lot with his almost proprioceptive hatred of everything Israeli and his passionate support of Hizbullah, Hamas, Syria and Iran. The same applies to Stanford's Noel Beinin who dines out on "Israeli war crimes," admires Jimmy Carter, and considers Hamas and Hezbollah as "heroes." Yosefa Loshitzky, formerly of the Hebrew University in Jerusalem and currently at the University of East London, suffers prominently for the Palestinians, signs Boycott Israel documents and spews hatred and falsehood on *The Electronic Intifada* website. And let us not forget the lamentable Charles Enderlin who, not content with fathering the al-Durah libel that has done untold harm to Israel and caused incalculable suffering, two years later published *Le rêve brisé: Histoire de l'échec du processus de paix au Proche-Orient (1995-2002)* in which Israel is blamed for scuppering the peace process.

Most recently, the Jewish South African jurist Richard Goldstone added his *shtick* to the dump-on-Israel movement. On September 16, 2009, Goldstone tabled his United Nations Report on Israeli conduct during Operation Cast Lead, accusing Israel of crimes it did not commit while effectively exculpating Hamas for crimes it did. Goldstone's strategy was initially to establish a moral equivalence between a country defending its citizens and a terrorist organization deliberately attacking that country's civilians. As one delves deeper into the Report, the strategy becomes ever more insidious, presenting Israel and Hamas not merely as moral equivalents but as political incompatibles, that is, Israel is depicted as a terrorist regime and Hamas as a legitimate government. Goldstone also implied that Israel, *but not Hamas*, might be referred to the International Criminal Court.

These are Jews who are made in the mold of Israel Shahak, friend of Edward Said, Noam Chomsky and Gore Vidal, and one of the most viperous Jewish Jew-haters of modern times. Their bible would be Shahak's anti-Talmudic and anti-Israeli *Jewish History, Jewish Tradition*. And their lineal ancestor, of course, is one Saul of Tarsus, who wrote of the Jews in *I Thessalonians* 2:15 that "they please not God, and are contrary to all men."

As for Israeli "revisionist historians," they have been Palestinian water-carriers for some time now. They too have made a major contribution toward the effort to disentitle their own country, one of the latest in the succession of ignominy being Tom Segev whose *Israel, The War, and the Year that Transformed the Middle East* faults the Jewish state for being over-hasty and paranoid in responding pre-emptively to the encroaching Arab armies and the illegal blockade of the Straits of Tiran to Israeli shipping. These are Jews who would likely not have survived to compose their books if the nation they so diligently traduce had not acted as it did, for as historian Michael Oren has affirmed, the original Arabic documents, detailing a certain "Operation Tariq" among others, show that Egypt, Syria and Jordan had planned "the expulsion or murder of much of [Israel's] Jewish inhabitants in 1967." These are Jews like Nahum Manbar who supplies Iran with technical knowledge and chemicals for its bioweapons industry and like Mordechai Vanunu who discloses sensitive information about Israel's defensive nuclear program in his opposition to the existence of a Jewish state. These are Jews like the aforementioned Ilan Pappe who, in an interview for *ynetnews.com* (March 15, 2008), promotes himself as a "great lover of the Palestinians," claims that the Palestinians "don't want to expel anyone" but only "to return while understanding that they will live alongside the Jews," and quite unbelievably asserts that "even people in Hamas" only wish to share the land.

These are the "wicked sons" and historical revisionists whom Steven Plaut of the University of Haifa has described as a "SWAT team for anti-Semites, and as apologists for Arab terror and Islamofascism"—the roster of these bullhorns for the antisemitic Left which he has listed on his blog, name after name after name, is almost beyond credence. Ephraim Karsh, too, has decisively debunked the sept of "New Historians" in sundry books and articles. What he has painstakingly shown of Benny Morris' former practice applies to the guild at large: "he misrepresents documents, resorts to partial quotes, withholds evidence, makes false assertions, and rewrites original documents." When it comes to the distortions and falsifications that "typify the New Historians' whole approach," he concludes, "the entire *raison d'être* of the historical discourse will have been lost"—unless the reason behind that discourse is to "invent an Israeli history in the image of their own choosing" (*The Middle East Quarterly*, Volume VI, Number 1). In purveying their mistranslations of the Hebrew archives and promoting outright fabrications, which Karsh has painstakingly brought to light, these ersatz historians are shameless advocates of Israeli "politicide" (*inFocus*, Spring 2008).

The Israeli media on the whole are equally begrimed, seeing as their mandate the shielding of the venal and irresponsible Labor/Kadima political establishment as if it were a Sukkot etrog—a symbiotic process that has come to be known as "etrog journalism" in which journalists protect and mollycoddle their favoured (Left) politicians like the ritual citrus. They have consistently manipulated their reporting to further political or personal complots, as Hanan Naveh, editor-in-chief of the Israel Broadcasting Authority, himself admitted at a Haifa University panel discussion: "We took it upon ourselves as a mission…to get the IDF out of Lebanon," since several of the news editors had sons serving there. The IBA also took it upon itself to downplay unwelcome items and events, to promote the Oslo fiasco, to smear those who opposed the Gaza disengagement, and to doctor newsclips in order to misrepresent political figures, like Benjamin Netanyahu, with whom it was not in sympathy. These are Jews like Ofer Nimrodi, publisher of the left-oriented mass circulation newspaper *Maariv*, convicted by an Israeli court on charges of plotting murder and of wiretapping. These are Jews who, like pitiable *Haaretz* columnist Gideon Levy, revile their own Prime Minister's rousing address to the UN on September 24, 2009 as "cheapening" the Holocaust and as "demagogic," and who refuse to fly the Israeli flag on Independence Day since they regard it, in Levy's words, as the "flag intended for provocation and confrontation." Or like his colleague Akiva Eldar who, in an epistolary exchange with Salameh Nematt of the *Al-Hayat* newspaper, accepted almost wholly the Palestinian reading of the conflict, laying the blame for the failed peace process on Israeli leaders rather than on the duplicity and rejectionism of Yasser Arafat. Another *Haaretz* poster boy, literary critic Yitzhak Laor, dissociates himself from the Israeli army, champions the fiercely anti-Israeli, late Palestinian laureate Mahmoud Darwish (who calls Jews "flying insects") and considers Israel as "the enemy."

They are well represented by their former editor David Landau who, at a dinner at the home of the American ambassador Richard Jones attended by Condoleezza Rice on September 10, 2007, called Israel a "failed state" that needed to be "raped" by the US. A month later, speaking at the Limmud Conference in Moscow, Landau happily admitted that he had "wittingly soft-pedalled" corruption allegations against Israeli prime ministers Ariel Sharon and Ehud Olmert to further the newspaper's peace agenda, in direct violation of the Israeli Press Council's ethics code. (Landau "stepped down" from his post in mid-February 2008—it may be that his dinner antics exceeded even this newspaper's editorial viewpoint.) These are Jews who, like the managing consortium of the same newspaper, distribute an *International Herald Tribune* ad taken out by The Nuclear Power and Development Company of Iran seeking tenders to build two large scale nuclear reactors in Bushehr province! The mind boggles. The Israeli media have, in effect, become a political party closely aligned with the manifold Left, in the same way as the American media have for the most part established themselves as an adjunct of the Democratic party. In effect, the Fourth Estate has become a fifth column.

It is also disturbing that such "rogue Jews" are often defended by those in the Reform/Reconstructionist communities and social pressure groups who purport to be reasonable and even-handed and who treat their declared enemies with forbearance. Indeed, if Reform/Reconstruction had been in place in fifth century B.C.E., Judaism would not have survived the Babylonian captivity. There would have been no Nehemiah to survey Jerusalem and formulate a plan for its restoration, no Ezra to lead the exiles back to the biblical homeland. There would, instead, have been lots of palaver and "dialogue," a sympathetic understanding of the Babylonian point of view, and a coming to terms with the existent situation.

One of the most instructive instances of this suicidal tendency to dodge and hedge, to dissemble the structure of reality, which should be kept in mind as a heuristic mnemonic, comes from the German-Jewish intellectual Franz Neumann. An intelligence analyst in the American OSS (Office of Strategic Services), Neumann wrote in his 1942 book, *Behemoth: The Structure and Practice of National Socialism*, "even though it may seem paradoxical, the German people are the least anti-Semitic [in Europe]." Neumann was a member of the emigré Frankfurt School and thus prone to speculative extravagance in which Jewish memory operated in only the most selective of ways, which makes him a prime object lesson for the contemporary Jew.

Then there are the teeming ranks of "good Jews"—those associated with a variety of blue-ribbon journals and prosperous institutions, especially in the United States, whose frequent, rosy, left-of-center tropism is a function of misremembrance. Bibliographic archives are notoriously underfunded in many prosperous Jewish communities. Holidays and lip-service are regarded as sufficient, but the documents relating to personal histories and family sagas, the records of commonplace suffering and of destitution overcome—the very grist of Diaspora experience—guaranteed by institutional memory are all too often left mouldering in library basements. Money is invested in architectural facades and glittering surfaces, as if exemplifying that old howler about the "edifice complex," rather than in archival vaults and muniments. The concern is chiefly with display; even the house of worship, I sometimes think, may be more appropriately described as a cinemagogue. The Jewish calendar is filled with festivals of remembering and yet for many Jews a kind of amnesia takes over once these holidays have passed. "Too many memorial days," writes Israeli poet Yehuda Amichai, "too little remembering."

As for the Prime Minister of Israel until his recent resignation, his former Chief of Staff and his Minister of Defense, it was Korah, Dathan and Abiram all over again, working against the very state they were sworn to protect.[11] Under such an administration, there could be no future for Israel: the country would be living from paycheck to paycheck. The last time in the history of Israel when it experienced a period of prolonged, if insecure, independence, commemorated in the Hannukah ritual, was during the one hundred year Hasmonean reign, which ended in the first century BCE. Thereafter, the power struggle between claimants to the throne led to the piecemeal dissolution of the state, the loss of territory and finally of its autonomy. Applying the Hasmonean scale, Israel today, at the age of 60-plus, would be a little more than halfway toward its denouement; but, prescinding from the conduct of its political and intellectual elite, the remaining years in the hypothetical progression may well telescope the calendar. According to the Hannukah story, the cruse of oil burned miraculously for eight days; the question now is whether it can burn for very much longer.

What hope can there be for a country whose Vice Premier and architect of the disastrous Oslo burlesque, Shimon Peres, falls asleep in the middle of a television interview while answering a question about the Iranian nuclear threat, or toadies before Saudi Arabia's King Abdullah at a UN podium, only to be unceremoniously rebuffed by the monarch? A country that awards the Emet Prize for Science, Art and Culture to former Hebrew University philosophy professor Avishai Margalit, who has made a sidebar career of slandering Israel in the

New York Review of Books for over twenty years? (Margalit has co-authored a rather interesting study, *Occidentalism: A Short History of Anti-Westernism*, with Ian Buruma who has since become one of Ayaan Hirsi Ali's most vehement detractors. There seems to be an inexplicable disconnect at work in the psyches of these writers.) What hope can there be for a country which permits the sale of hundreds of dunams of rich agricultural land in the Galilee to Arab tycoons? Or allows the family of Ala Abu Dhaim, who murdered eight yeshiva students in cold blood before being shot dead, to raise a mourning tent and hoist Hizbullah and Hamas flags in the middle of East Jerusalem, reconsidering only some time later?—most ironically, it was Jordan that prohibited public mourning for the slain terrorist.

And what future can there be for a country whose academic and human rights organizations lend their name to what, on the evidence, is nothing short of a subversive undertaking? The Association for Civil Rights in Israel (ACRI) has refused to demand the return of Israel's abducted soldiers or that they be granted the right to visits from the Red Cross. Gisha, the Legal Center for Freedom of Movement, accuses the State of prohibiting Palestinian students from Gaza from studying at Israeli universities. The latter group has drafted a letter, signed by many left-wing luminaries, protesting the "boycott," focusing on a Palestinian doctoral candidate in Chemistry. That no Israeli student would be permitted to study in Gaza or could hope to survive the venture, that Gaza is effectively at war with Israel, and that chemical knowledge is used in Gaza for manufacturing explosives and improving rocket propellant are apparently issues of no importance. The example of Awad al-Qiq, killed by an Israeli air strike, is instructive in this regard. A science professor at a United Nations school in Gaza by day, he applied his know-how to building rockets at night as "the chief leader" of Islamic Jihad's "engineering unit" (*Reuters*, May 5, 2008). Gisha would be better advised to learn from American law enforcement, which recently arrested two Egyptian Engineering students at the University of South Florida for using their expertise to build explosive devices.

Gisha subsequently released a report faulting Israel for "ruining the economy of the Gaza Strip" and for continuing the "occupation" by controlling border crossings—this in the face of the indisputable facts that the Hamas government is a terrorist phalanx, that an overwhelming majority of Gazans voted it into office, a*nd that U.N. Security Council binding Resolution 1373, passed under Chapter VII of the U.N. Charter on September 28, 2001, explicitly stipulates that all states must "prevent the movement of terrorists or terrorist groups by effective border controls."* Gisha acted as it did fully aware of Hamas' terrorist charter (embellished by the famous hadith calling for Muslims to hasten the Day of Judgment by killing Jews) and its overt declaration of war with Israel, and that unguarded border crossings are an open sesame to kidnappers and suicide bombers. A milder form of such unpardonable naivety was furnished by our old friend *Haaretz* columnist Akiva Eldar who, in a talk delivered at the Jewish Public Library to the Canadian Friends of Peace Now in Montreal on September 25, 2007, confidently asserted that Hamas—which, to repeat, is by its own admission and constant example unflaggingly committed to violence and the total annihilation of the Jewish state—will come to accept Israel and a lasting concordat since "it will have to take into account public opinion." This is reminiscent of Israeli novelist David Grossman's slogan, "peace of no choice," which would immediately deprive him of it. The mind continues to boggle.

A good example of the fecklessness of Israeli political life in general is furnished by the Winograd Commission, delegated to investigate Israel's poor performance in the summer 2006 war and determine the responsibility of its military and political leaders, whose members were handpicked by the Prime Minister himself—the report delivered a verdict that, unflattering as it was, enabled a failed Israeli leadership to remain in power. Another is the "Geneva Accord" signed by Israeli Tweedledees like Amos Oz and Yossi Beilin and their Palestinian Tweedledums, Nibal Kassis and Yasser Abed Rabbo (the same Rabbo who, as head of the Palestinian negotiating team, rejected the 2001 Clinton parameters that the Israelis had accepted). Beilin, former leader of the Meretz Party, is on record asserting that the early Zionists should have accepted the British offer of a state in Uganda, and continues to write and argue as if peace were an acceptable substitute for survival. That an "accord" which would constrict the bargaining power of the Israeli government while giving away the country's defensible borders, bringing Tel Aviv into the range of even homemade rockets and enabling a mechanized army to cut Israel in two, does not appear to signify. These starry-eyed peacemongers are quite unable to see that their piece of paper would deliver only a peace of paper.

No less distressing is the hands-off treatment long accorded the Israeli-Arab representatives who sit in the Knesset. These MKs, many of whom openly sided with Hizbullah during the summer 2006 war, colluded with Syria and called for the kidnapping of IDF soldiers, are now summoning "Muslims and Arabs" to "liberate" Jerusalem (to quote Ibrahim Sarsour of the UAL-Ta'al party) and agitating for an international boycott *of their own country*. In nations that are politically mature, such acts are known as treason. In countries that are fighting for their very existence, such acts are dealt with summarily. In Israel, the enemy is tolerated, lest he be offended and the international community aggrieved.

Such timorous retreats before the imperatives of duty and reason may be observed even on the level of the treatment of the common individual. Thus Yifat Alkobi, a member of the embattled community of 600 Jews living in Hebron with its 120,000 Arabs, was accused by the international press and detained by the Israeli police for verbally abusing a Palestinian woman, but nothing is said about the bullet holes that reportedly pock every caravan in her neighbourhood. Indeed, the fact that Alkobi's house has been strafed by Palestinian snipers for years, that her daughter was nearly killed by a terrorist's bullet, and that her use of an off-colour epithet was occasioned by a physical assault has somehow gone largely unreported. (It was in Hebron, in the anti-Jewish riots of 1929, that 67 Jewish men, women and children were butchered and the Jewish community expelled.) Similarly, Israeli sheep farmer Shai Dromi was arrested for shooting and killing a Bedouin thief who had poisoned his guard dogs and was in the act of stealing his flock—the fourth such attempt on the farm. Dromi was remanded into custody under the pending charge of manslaughter, yet until recently little was done by the police and left-leaning judiciary to curtail the Bedouin criminal gangs which roam the Israeli Negev, for obvious political—or politically correct—reasons.[12] Bowing to public pressure, the Knesset finally passed the "Shai Dromi Bill" in June 2008 allowing property owners to use fatal force against thieves and intruders. Naturally, the bill was opposed by the left-wing and Arab parties, such as Meretz and the United Arab List. Dromi was acquitted of the manslaughter charges but sentenced to five months of community service for illegal possession and use of a weapon.

These may be small narratives in the larger scheme of things but they are profound expressions of the stent between the personal and the political, testifying to the cloud of self-delegitimation that has descended over much of the country. Israel's left-wing media, politicians, intellectuals and "peace organizations" have been exceedingly sedulous in leading the charge against their own and setting the country on auto-destruct—Israeli kapos in good standing.[13] As a typical example, we have, once again, the Association for Civil Rights in Israel which highlights "discriminatory practices" against Arab-Israelis, taking their brief against Israel as far as the UN's Committee on the Elimination of Racial Discrimination. Yet, as we have seen, it ignores entirely the terror context in which Israel must maneuver and the measures necessary to reduce the incidence of suicide bombings, drive-by shootings, and rocket attacks upon civilian centers. It had nothing to say about Hamas operatives using the premises of an UNRWA (United Nations Relief and Works Agency) school in Beit Hanun to shell Israeli towns and cities, banking on the Israeli reluctance to target civic centers. It also had nothing to say about those Jewish-Israeli citizens prosecuted by their own government for defending themselves against Arab threats to their persons and property. It does not address the dilemma of Arab Christians living in Bethlehem and other Palestinian cities gradually being driven out by the Muslim majority, and has refused to condemn the illegal abduction and detention by Hamas and Hizbullah of Israeli soldiers Gilad Shalit, Udi Goldwasser and Elded Regev. (The latter two, it now turns out, were killed during the initial Hizbullah raid, their mutilated bodies having been returned in the July 2008 "prisoner exchange.") Its latest *démarche* has been to file an appeal with the Israeli Supreme Court protesting the stringency of airport security checks that focus on Israeli Arabs, though who else might carry explosive materials aboard an El Al flight originating at Ben Gurion airport remains moot, to say the least.

Another case in point: Tel Aviv University's Faculty of Law hosted a conference on January 8, 2007, in which imprisoned terrorists were redefined as "political prisoners." One such terrorist, recently released from an Israeli jail, was given a place of honour at the podium. Tali Fahima, the Israeli leftist activist who had been convicted of collaborating with Zakaria Zubeidi, chief of the al-Aqsa Martyrs' Brigades in Jenin, was also an honoured guest. Another session dealt with the hardships suffered by the families of Palestinian terrorists. The victims of these terrorists were not so much as mentioned and no reference was made to the soldiers abducted by the Islamic militias and held in violation of international law or of the hardships endured by *their* families.

Following Operation Cast Lead, another treasonous group appeared on the scene, calling itself Breaking The Silence. Funded in part by Britain, Holland and the EU bureaucracy, it falsely accuses Israel of having used Gazan civilians as human shields and of wantonly destroying houses—without presenting hard and fast evidence for its claims. Its report collects the affidavits of 54 soldiers, *all of whom are anonymous*, and relies largely on second-hand information. Similarly, the self-styled Rabbis for Human Rights held a conference at the Van Leer Institute in Jerusalem in late July 2009 castigating the IDF for its activities in Gaza. RHR is funded by Trocaire, an Irish Catholic group with an overt bias against Israel, and allegations have arisen that Spain is also implicated.

As for the vociferous and influential Peace Now movement (which I have elsewhere dubbed the War Later movement and which Israel's Vice Premier has rightly diagnosed as "a virus"), it has opposed almost every Israeli measure to defend the country against its enemies and has laboured to frustrate even its peacetime initiatives. In November 2006, Peace Now published a report condemning Israel for undertaking construction of the Ma'aleh Adumim settlement near Jerusalem on 86% of privately owned Palestinian land. In March 2007, it was forced by the facts to correct its estimate—the 86% turned into

.5%. Some may argue that even half a percent is too much, but the issue is rectifiable and comes under the jurisdiction of the Israeli Supreme Court which has consistently ruled in favour of Palestinian interests (as it did, for instance, when it cancelled a law exempting the State from liability for collateral damages to Palestinians in the conduct of anti-terrorist operations, thereby hampering the efforts of its own army to protect its own citizens). On April 29, 2007, the General Secretary of the movement, Yariv Oppenheimer, posted a blog in which he urged Israelis to take seriously "the calls for peace from Syria and the Saudi initiative"—which would mean, in real-world terms, the loss of the Golan Heights and the return of the millions of meretricious refugees, which is to say, the imminent end of the Jewish state. On June 26, this same Oppenheimer posted yet another blog suggesting that Israel begin negotiations with the renegade Hamas government, open the border crossings and allow Gazan labourers into Israel in order to give Gaza "a chance to recuperate"—one can imagine the suicide bombers and guerilla fighters streaming in under cover of shovel and pick, though Oppenheimer plainly cannot. Oppenheimer also seems indifferent to the fact that it is Hamas and not Israel that is keeping the Kerem Shalom border crossing closed as a matter of official policy, as Hamas spokesman Fawzi Barhoum affirmed on July 7, 2007, and that mortar barrages are one of the means it is employing.

One of Peace Now's most recent escapades was to hang Syrian flags on the Jerusalem road, arguably an act of treason since Israel has been in a state of war with Syria since the latter's invasion of 1973. That Syria had been cooperating with North Korea in the construction of a Yongbyon-model uranium-extraction plant at the Al Kibar facility in Deir al Zour, a fact that can no longer be doubted, does not appear to have enlightened the group to the danger it is courting. Propaganda mules such as Peace Now are incapable of learning from either history or experience—Palestinians stoned a Peace Now bus carrying a delegation which had come to Hebron to join a pro-Palestinian, "anti-settler" demonstration! No matter. Peace Now drives on. No mention of the fact that Hebron is an ancient Jewish community and, apart from this, that the land in question was legally purchased by Spanish Sephardim in the 16th century. No mention of the fact that Palestinian

Arabs are building whole villages in the Galilee and the Negev without building permits and on land poached from the state. Indeed, there is no acknowledgement of the fact that, despite the forcible dislocations of history, Jews have striven to remain on their land since earliest times—for example, in Jerusalem, in Safed, in Tiberias, in Tzipori, in Hebron, and in Peki'in where they have lived since the destruction of the Second Temple in 70 C.E. except for a brief period between 1936-1948 when they suffered expulsion at the hands of Arab and Druse mobs.

A large number of Israelis, well-intentioned and influential, seem to have downloaded the road map to national suicide, indifferent to the fact that the people they want to help are the people who want to dhimmify and even to destroy them. It was a covey of Palestinian sympathizers and Arab intellectuals who objected to the appearance of three internationally famous, left-wing, pro-disengagement Israeli writers at the 2008 Turin book fair. Amos Oz, David Grossman and A.B. Yehoshua, who have been uniformly critical of Israeli policies and are stalwart supporters of the movement to create a Palestinian state, seem blissfully unaware that, for the Left in general and Palestinians in particular, convictions do not matter as much as entelechy. They are Jewish and Israeli. As the *Jerusalem Post* commented after the Mumbai massacre in November 2008, in which Chabad House was attacked and its occupants murdered in cold blood, "the terrorists did not inquire whether their victims were haredi, Orthodox, traditional or secular." In the minds of their oppugners, being Jewish is sufficient to disqualify them not only from attending a book fair but from remaining members of the human family. Nevertheless, many Jews continue to pursue the Fata(h) Morgana of concord and kinship with those who will never accept them regardless of the painful and risky concessions to the "Other" they are willing to make.

They do not seem to understand that the Jewish nation is in deep trouble and that the Arabs can afford to wait. After all, the Arabs have oil. The Arabs have the tergiversators of the West with them—the multicultural liberals, the unnatural creatures of the ubiquitous feminist sorority who multiply on university campuses, the squalid mainstream media, and the anti-democratic left *en masse*. The Arabs have the universal animus against Jews as their greatest and most effective collaborator. And they have the peace-befuddled and soft-minded Israeli left tunneling as a Fifth Column on their behalf.

Regrettably, cognitive dissonance never stopped a zealot.

10

A Most Disturbing Case

Wunderkind Naomi Klein, who has made a name for herself as a one-woman anti-Israeli bulldozer, is another of these turncoat Jews putting her equipment in the service of the country's enemies, and one of the most influential. This has become her logo. In a column for *The Guardian* (June 16, 2007), she accuses Israel of having cynically profited from the state of terror in which it finds itself, "selling fences to an apartheid planet" along with a host of surveillance devices like unmanned drones, biometric IDs and prisoner interrogation systems, "precisely the tools and technologies Israel has used to lock in the occupied territories." Israel, she claims, "has learned to turn endless war into a brand asset," using its *soi-disant* oppression of the Palestinian people as an exercise in pioneering the means to industrialize "the global war on terror" and to fatten on the rich contracts generated by these innovations. (This position is growing ever more commonplace; in her new book, *Failing Peace*, Sara Roy claims that Israelis are reaping the benefits of the "occupation" in the form of a robust economy.)

For Klein, Israel has become a homeland security Megacorp for whom the Palestinians are merely "guinea pigs" in the testing of new instruments of detection, control and persecution—"something to keep in mind in the debates about the academic boycott." In developing her astigmatic thesis, Klein makes no mention of Israel's withdrawal from southern Lebanon in 2000 or its unilateral disengagement from Gaza in 2005, of Israel's need to defend itself from constant attack by an enemy sworn to the country's complete destruction or of the Damoclean sword of nuclear annihilation that hangs over it. She does not speak of Ayatollah Akbar Hashemi Rafsanjani's twice-uttered threat to launch a nuclear attack against Israel, taken up more recently by Mahmoud Ahmadinejad, the modern incarnation of the biblical Haman. But Klein is no Esther. I have yet to hear her comment upon the latest instance of this menace, General Mohammad Ali Jaafari, commander of the Iranian Revolutionary Guards, promising to destroy the "cancerous bacterium" of Israel by "radiation" treatment.

From her vantage point, terrorism does not exist as such but is a Western and Israeli fabrication, the corollary of an informational covin whose purpose is to maximize profits at the expense of the world's dispossessed and downtrodden peoples. Never mind 9/11, never mind London, Madrid, Bali, Nairobi, never mind Iran, Syria and Hizbullah, never mind the Hamas bloodbath in Gaza, never mind the Kassam rockets falling like clockwork on Israeli towns, never mind *truly* courageous writers like Salman Rushdie, Ayaan Hirsi Ali, Ibn Warraq, Steven Emerson, Fiamma Nirenstein and many other real and potential victims of the Islamic fatwa—all of these are only by-products of the corporate merger of the Western imagination and the Western entrepreneurial impulse, what she calls "disaster capitalism," an invented phenomenon which ensures her best-seller status. The fact that China, Russia and North Korea are among the world's leading exporters of sophisticated weaponry, which has nothing to do with "capitalism" as she understands it (she gives Russia, victimized by the West, a minor bye), leaves her unfazed, as does her own literary profiteering and self-commodification on the back of the very industry she deplores.

As for Israel, the "constant state of fear" in which it lives is, apparently, nothing short of an exploitable godsend, the country's "ultimate renewable resource." It appears that Klein has never heard of economist Frédéric Bastiat's celebrated "fallacy of the broken window," developed in his 1850 work *That Which Is Seen and that Which Is Unseen*, which makes it evident that prosperity based upon policies inviting destruction is counter-productive. Israel knows this. In point of fact, Israel's greatest resource is the high intellectual capacity of an educated citizenry and its world-class scientific establishment. As Klein should know, Israel's chief exports are by no means exclusively military—the profits from which represent only a small fraction of its total GDP—but derive from the fields of advanced cybernetics, desalination projects, hydrology, energy technology, productive agricultural methods and life-saving medical technology, in all of which it is among the world's acknowledged leaders.

In fact three quarters of Israel's annual $70 billion export trade reside in the high-tech sector. Cisco Technology has poured more than $1 billion into Israeli companies, in which Microsoft is also heavily invested. Windows XP, Vista and Microsoft Office were all developed in Israel. Virus protection software and firewalls, cellphones, voice mail, instant messaging devices, Intel microchips and Pentium microprocessors were also developed in Israel. IBM maintains three R & D Centers in the country and Google two, including the largest research lab outside the United States; in fact, Google runs on Israeli search algorithms. Continuing the tradition, Google's new super-search algorithm, Orion, launched on March 24, 2009, was developed by an Israeli doctoral student, Ori Allon. One of Israel's newest technological breakthroughs involves the Mobile Internet, where it is once again a global forerunner. The multi-jacketed Modu cellphone, which has made the *Guinness Book of Records*, has brought user functionality to a new level, unmatched anywhere in the world. The first wireless LAN (Local Area Network) was developed in Israel. Nowhere is such information referenced or made room for in Klein's work, for from her peculiar perspective, no doubt, such cutting-edge expertise would constitute further evidence for Israel's exploitation of a ravaged planet. Given Israel's dominance in the informatic world, I would expect that, to avoid complicity in composing her texts, Klein must write with a quill and communicate by carrier pigeon.

The Israeli "brand" is one that creates value for humankind. Klein neglects to mention, for example, that Israel's universities are rated among the best in the world, graduating a higher number of scientists and engineers per capita than any other country, that it has produced eight Nobel laureates to date, that it generates more scientific paper per capita than any other country, or that the Israeli pharmaceutical company, Teva, is the world's foremost supplier of antibiotic medicines, including its "flagship drug" Copaxone which treats Multiple Sclerosis. Had she done her homework, Klein would have been aware that the Community Research and Development Information Service (CORDIS) has ranked Israel at the forefront of alternative energy R & D, with over 200 firms specializing in environmental and energy-related technology (January 12, 2005). She would have had to acknowledge the Weizmann Institute's bioinformatics computer project that will enable Eastern Europe and Asia to access the online molecular biology resource network, which even UNESCO has singled out for praise. She would have recognized that the Institute is also involved in the high-profile SESAME Project ("Synchrotron-light Experimental Science and Applications in the Middle-East") to produce high-energy light streams for physical experiments, an initiative which envisions the cooperation of Arab scientists. She would have known that a partnership of Israeli and American companies are building the largest solar power plant of the last quarter century (*BusinessWeek*, February 14, 2006) and that "Israeli technology built nine solar plants in southern California...eliminating the need for nearly two million barrels of oil each year" (*solel.com*, June19, 2006). She would have known that the Ariva Power Company is one of the most advanced solar enterprises in the world, working towards the preparation of large-scale megawatt fields, an exportable technology. She would have mentioned that Israel has offered to desalinate water to redress Jordan's critical shortage and that half of Europe's water technology programs involve Israeli companies. A boycott against Israel would be a European catastrophe. Any of a number of easily accessible sources would have informed her that Israel's Epcon Industries is a world pioneer in wind-turbine technology; that the AORA company is beginning construction of the world's first hybrid solarized gas turbine power station which runs on solar energy by day and biofuel by night; and that Ormat Industries is opening up the field of geothermal energy, operating eleven plants in five countries, servicing over half a million people, and is currently constructing a 340-megawatt geothermal power project in Indonesia.

If she were interested, she would note that Israeli geneticist Karen Avraham of Tel Aviv University has carried out important research into microRNA molecules that regulate gene expression and protein production, promising a cure for deafness, whether age-related or genetic (*Proceedings of the National Academy of Sciences*, or PNAS, April, 2009). And that it is in Israel that a new biomarker, called placental protein 13 (PP13), a pre-diagnostic for various severe fetal diseases, has been developed (*Jerusalem Post*, May 23, 2009). Should Klein ever fall ill with internal organ diseases, would she reject the application of Israel's newest medical technology, the world's tiniest medical video camera developed by two Israeli companies, Megidus and Tower Semiconductor, to be used for disposable endoscopes? (*Arutz Sheva News*, August 4, 2009). Were she honest and consistent, she would have to refuse to be treated with such state-of-the-art devices.

All of which prompts the query: Is Klein guilty of inexcusable ignorance as a scholar and commentator or simply of the willful suppression of facts we expect of the propagandist or the bigot? Her venomous account of Israel's purposes and practices has about the same degree of truth-value as the reports in two Palestinian newspapers, *Al-Ayyam* and *Al-Hayat Al-Jadida*, on July 17 and 18, 2008, respectively, that Israel has released giant rats immune to poison into the streets of Jerusalem in order to "turn the residents' life into a living hell, forcing them to leave" (*Al-Ayyam*). The reports do not explain how the rats are able to distinguish between Arab and Jew, no more than Klein is able to discriminate between truth and fiction.

We know that Klein is an advocate of green technology. One wonders how serious she can be since, relative to Israel, she spares the saprophytic countries of the Muslim Middle East where fortunes are made on the exploitation of fossil fuels. But if we give her the benefit of the doubt, what would she then make of the fact that Israel is now working toward the development of an environment-friendly electric car network, which it plans to have fully operational by 2011; Israel Corp. is also a world pace-setter in "green electricity," which will supply the power for this venture, called Project Better Place. None of this is mentioned by Klein who is engaged in her own particular venture, which we might dub Project Worst Place. Were she compiling her decretals today, I suspect there would be no reference to the fact that, punching far above its weight, tiny Israel ranked seventh in the number of by-country competitive research grants awarded by the European Union or that the World Economic Forum rated Israel as 17th out of 125 countries in its 2007 Global Competitive Index. But expurgation is the only way she can support her biased and hypertrophic argument, elaborated at greater length in her new book, *The Shock Doctrine: The Rise of Disaster Capitalism*, in which, as it happens, a Jewish economist, Milton Friedman, is damned for most of the contemporary world's ills. (That this farrago of lies, slander and poor scholarship was recently awarded the $90,000 Warwick Prize for Writing is only an indication of how far the intellectual world has fallen from the benchmarks of good judgment, common sense and educated cultivation.)

Klein also seems to have forgotten that Israel, a legitimate nation, has been carded by much of the world since its inception and has been forced to fight a war for very survival from the day it was recognized by the United Nations. It has never once in its brief history initiated a war of pure aggression—even the Suez War was preceded by Egypt's closing the Suez Canal to Israeli shipping and blockading the Gulf of Aqaba in violation of the longstanding Constantinople Convention. Its weapons have been used in self-defense against an enemy that has never ceased to plot its annihilation by the entire gamut of available means, political, economic or military. To argue, as Klein does, that Israel "field-tests" its arsenal-for-export against a defenseless, subject population and therefore wishes to prolong the conflict, cultivating its own precariousness among its bellicose neighbours merely to stimulate the economy, is not only totally wacky and sophistical. It is high slander and a form of intellectual marauding, an act of invidious defamation suggesting both ignorance and spite.

So far as I can see, obliquity seems to run in the family, as it does among the Jewish people itself. Klein's husband, Avi Lewis, a fairly muscular Leftist interviewer for the Canadian Broadcasting Corporation, has departed the already highly-politicized Mother Corp for the Big Leagues: Al-Jazeera, which calls suicide bombers "martyrs," which hosts the anti-Jewish, jihadist-backing Sheikh Yusuf al-Qaradawi's "Islamic Law and Life" radio show, and which has been shilling for al-Qaeda since the early 1990s. Lewis' first coup for his new boss, Sheikh Hamad bin Khalifi al-Thani of Qatar, was to deride Cuban-Americans who tend to vote conservative Republican and to urge a shift toward the socialist-left Democratic party. (Lewis was recently joined by his former boss at the CBC, Tony Burman, who has left the Canadian farm team to be named director of Al-Jazeera's English language operations.)

Should Israel disappear, either through internal fission or attack from without, or both, these are the people who will bear the responsibility and the guilt. "One can either…associate one's Jewishness with all the negativism history…has appended to it," wrote the Jewish Canadian poet A. M. Klein (no relation to Naomi) to his American counterpart Karl Shapiro, "or one can feel oneself…as part of a great tradition…whose fruitfulness is by no means exhausted." The first option is unfortunately all too frequent. A.M. Klein makes his case most powerfully in an unfinished novel, *Stranger and Afraid*, where he writes: "Ignoble and base is he who forsakes the weak in whose midst he finds himself to go over…to the camp of the strong. It is treachery. It is a coward's choice. It is a despicable desertion. Its perpetrator ceases to be not only a Jew, but a man." Or a woman. But self-rejection will render such Jews no less exposed to their enemies than self-assertion, transforming them not into soaring doves but sitting ducks. For these are Jews who appear to have learned absolutely nothing from the history of dereliction and slaughter which is their long inheritance. For them, memory is a gaping hole.

11

The Question

The question must be posed. Why are Jews—not all, of course, but a truly disconcerting number—so prone to turn against themselves and make common cause with those who, given the chance, would delight in their extermination? Have they interiorized the antisemite's evaluation of their presumed unworthiness? Is this the real meaning of "assimilation," the absorption into the plasm of Jewish cultural and intellectual life of a microbial pathogen? Despite the fury and indignation with which many in the Jewish community greeted the publication of Kenneth Levin's *The Oslo Syndrome* (the Jewish/Israeli variant of the Stockholm Syndrome), its thesis seems persuasive. The Jewish people, he contends, suffer an inheritance of guilt, having brought aboard the perennial Gentile calumny regarding their tainted "substance" as an ethnic collectivity, so that they have gradually come to see themselves through the eyes of their traducers. This act of psychic displacement has taken hold in the Jewish soul, variously leading it to shrink in self-abasement, to retire into the shell of subdued anonymity, to do everything in its power not to call attention to itself, to suffer indignities quietly, to suspect its own motivations, to accept the scriptures of a demonic inquisition and to attack itself at last like an immune system gone awry.

The fearful Jew, as I have pointed out above, tends to transpose the fight against injustice to other nations and communities, pressing for the rights not of Israeli Jews but Palestinian Arabs and Sudanese animists. Thus he consolidates his fugitive merit. The reprobate Jew, however, takes his "idealism" to the next level of self-effacement, reversing the sign of his object. He struggles against injustice by reprehending not Palestinian terrorists and Sudanese Janjaweed but Israeli Jews themselves whose right to security, whose national legitimacy and whose suffering, courage and ethical stamina—despite the inevitable and ramifying exceptions to the rule and the moral flaws intrinsic to the human condition as such—he perceives as an affront and does everything in his power to misrepresent as its opposite. But both the reasonable Jew and the irrational Jew work against their own long-term interests in a pusillanimous and delinquent flight before the Accuser.

Millennia of social and cultural quarantine must have their effect on the sensibility of a people, producing a creature who is always in danger of becoming reflexively disenchanted or of contracting that wasting disease which Ruth Wisse in *Jews and Power* has called "the veneration of political weakness." Only the strong survive themselves. One thinks of that memorable scene in novelist Paul Scott's *Raj* series, in which a scorpion, trapped in a ring of fire, coils up with the heat and appears to sting itself with its own lethal tail. Analogously, surrounded by the flames of enmity, misprision and commination, the weak-spirited Jew shrivels back upon himself, the autonomic convulsion of an ailing and enervated soul. But he goes even further, anticipating his own demise by self-administering the *piqûre de grâce*, doing the work of his tormentors as if in agreement with their salvos of defilement and vilification. He may even delude himself into believing that the high conception of justice inherent in the Jewish faith requires him to decry the Zionist enterprise which is its flickering and terrestrial fulfillment, if not to renounce that very faith itself. By a bizarre act of metaphysical commutation, the self-despising Jew becomes the antisemite's loyal deputy, assuming liability for the world's mortal caricature of him and willing his own eclipse. It's a kind of solution, after all.

But the bare bodkin may probe even more deeply. Living as the Jew does in a psychological ghetto, perhaps this tendency to inflict a wound upon the body of his people is the one area in which he can still experience his freedom—that is, by volunteering before being conscripted, in short, by denying himself and thereby eradicating the stigma of his nature. He exits the *mellah* by rejecting wholly what he is and profaning the kinship which defines him—not only within his own soul but for the world at large. Only by raising his hand against his own may he finally shed the manacles which bind them. Or so he believes. This, at least, the world will permit him to do, and even applaud him for it, if only for a time. Blind to how ephemeral is his moment in the sun, he feels he has achieved both liberty and approval at last. In this way, self-hatred turns surreptitiously into the long-awaited emancipation of the diseased. But what sort of freedom is this? Swallowing poison in the conviction that it is the most effective kind of medication can have only one practical result: the freedom from pain implicit in self-extinction, which is not genuine freedom but only surcease.

Nevertheless, the recreant Jew persists in the belief that he need no longer see himself as the golem from which the society of mankind has recoiled but as a heroic warrior who willingly fights on its behalf, receiving as a reward for self-immolation his desired pardon, his long-deferred manumission and his crowning enfranchisement. In an effort to shape his condition and remake his destiny, he believes that by kissing the Gentile princess, if she will graciously permit, he will be magically transformed into the shining avatar of communal redemption. Or alternately, by having the slipper fit, the scullery maid is changed into a royal personage. Thus it is that renegade Jews are always happy to become token Jews, showcased at antisemitic seminars, congresses and fora. They pose as rabid anti-Zionists, but their anti-Zionism is nothing more or less than a kosher antisemitism. In so being and doing, they acquire what historian Robert Wistrich calls "historic dissident status" by willfully providing their enemies with the ammunition they need to advance their cause while disguising their intentions. "Anti-Semites rely on Jews to confirm their prejudice," writes Emanuele Ottolenghi, for "if Jews recur to such language and advocate such policies, how can anyone be accused of anti-Semitism for making the same arguments?" This is the "mechanism through which an anti-Semitic accusation becomes respectable"(*National Review*, September 20, 2006).

Let us call these perjurious specimens Theobald-Jews. According to the Benedictine monk Thomas of Monmouth in his *The Life and Miracles of St. William of Norwich* (1173), it was an apostate Jew, a certain Theobald, who, swore that Jews had killed twelve-year old William, a tanner's apprentice, to fulfill their "Passover blood ritual" in the fateful year of 1144—the first recorded such episode in a long line of murderous defamations. As a matter of interest, the paradigm of ritual-murder accusation goes back at least to 40 B.C.E. when, as we read in the *Contra Apion* of Flavius Josephus, the antisemitic grammarian Apion accused the Jews of Alexandria of slaughtering a Greek man, "lying upon a bed in the temple," for the purposes of ritual cannibalism. "How is it possible," Josephus asks, "that the entrails of one man should be sufficient for so many thousands of Jews to taste, as Apion pretends?" But antisemitic logic has never been especially profound or intelligible. "It is a great shame," Josephus concludes, "for a grammarian not to be able to write a true history." But the shame is shared by many.

The *blood libel* as such, however, seems to be a medieval Christian invention, fostered with the help of those who were, or who were once, part of the Jewish community itself. Apostate Jews were at the source of many of the blood libels in the medieval period and, *mutatis mutandis*, they are still with us today. The world is teeming with Theobald-Jews who are ready to traduce their own people to serve what they regard as their advantage, or as an expression of their own self-loathing, and in the process cater to the ammoniac hatred of the current brood of crypto-antisemites posing as anti-Zionists. "These words—observe, the words of a converted Jew—we reckon to be all the truer," wrote Thomas of Monmouth, "in that we received them as uttered by one who was a converted enemy."

In today's world, of course, conversion is no longer necessary; compliance will do. The value of the turncoat is well understood by the anti-Israel organizations which co-opt him or her. A timely example has just been afforded by the pro-boycott, anti-Zionist University and College Union in the U.K., which has created a Facebook page in order to build, according to its spokesman Mike Cushman, an international network of "anti-Zionist Jews to support Palestinian resistance and seed new Jewish anti-Zionist organizing." The apostate Jew, the *apikoros*, who confers legitimacy on the campaign against Jewish interests or the state of Israel, is the antisemite's most effective weapon. Even the word "antisemitism" was coined by an apostate, the half-Jew William Marr whose 1879 pamphlet, *The Victory of Judaism over Germanism*, launched the modern, race-based antisemitic movement.

There is not much doubt that what we are observing is a pathology of the first magnitude, what the Talmudic sages called *sin'at akhim*, or brotherly hatred, an element of Jewish life sufficiently pronounced to merit a name of its own. There is something in this species of Jews that hates the Jew in them, that recoils in disgust and self-contempt before the image of themselves they see in their fellow Jews, or before the reflection of themselves when they look in the soul's mirror. It is almost as if they have internalized Koranic surah 5:64 which says of Jews that "They spread evil and corruption in the land." This degree of self-abhorrence must be nearly unprecedented, for rarely, if ever, has an ethnic or national collective turned against an entire nation made up of people with whom it shares an ancestral tradition and a millennial archive. History furnishes many examples of a social or intellectual group targeting a *particular class* of a society with which it is in one way or another associated or identified. But to defame an *entire country* with whose inhabitants one shares a cultural or genealogical relation, to dispute its founding principles, to cast suspicion upon its moral character, to support its enemies and to question its right to existence is surely a unique phenomenon. Even those Germans horrified by the abominations of the Nazis, or Russians sickened by the excesses of the Communists, rarely went to the extremes of repudiation and proscription evinced by the truants of the Jewish faith.

Arthur Koestler has said that, for the Jew, treason is the highest form of patriotism. There is a deep insight kernelled in this aphorism that needs some unpacking. Because the Jew is schooled to believe that Judaism incarnates the quintessence of morality and that Israel must be, as the prophet Isaiah proclaimed, a light unto the nations, any falling away from this supernal principle is regarded as an inexpiable transgression. Such Jews cannot tolerate raw humanity, the "human, all too human" blemish in our nature, and for this reason they will contemn their own people when they fail to exemplify so exalted an imperative toward moral perfection as inscribed in the prophetic literature and the tablets of the law.

We might say that he suffers a perverted form of the Masada complex, committing suicide on the crest of the ideal in order to avoid surrendering to himself. The irony is that this is the Jew who lapses or sets his face against his own because he subscribes to the very idea of chosenness that he brusquely disavers. He is a common human type, of course, the moral invertebrate who cannot bear or digest disappointment and seeks to avenge what he interprets as a broken covenant. He candles his eggs and erroneously concludes they are infertile. The fluttering birth of promise is trumped by the hankering for angel's wings. For having placed his faith in the distinction of the impossible, he has come to feel *failed by*, like a child who discovers his mother is not perfect. Only, in the frame of reference we are considering here, his tantrum of resentment has vaster and unexpected repercussions. Such is the Jewish family romance: the Jew who betrays his people feels betrayed by his people. Thus the ideal, which cannot be fully maintained in this world but to which he cleaves in all the puerility of his innocence, becomes the source of his guilt. And thus disgrace becomes a function of assumed pre-eminence.

And yet, in denouncing his own, the Jew who has succumbed to this noxious contagion does not actually realize that he is sabotaging and effectively annulling the only life he has, that is, the life that history has scripted for him and which, despite the conviction of his own free will and individual autonomy, he can no more recant than Hamlet can sue for Norwegian citizenship. The play does not allow for it. Regardless of what he may think or wish, a Jew cannot "opt out," like the protagonist of Michael Chabon's *The Yiddish Policemen's Union* who abjures the "sandal-wearing idiot whose claim to fame is that he was ready to cut his own son's throat for the sake of a hare-brained idea" and who considers that his homeland is his hat and his ex-wife's tote bag. He has forgotten that the Jewish sense of security is always a false sense of security, that over the past 2000 years, as Melvin Konner points out in *Unsettled: An Anthropology of the Jews*, Jews have been expelled from 94 countries, and does not think to ask himself why the future should be any different. In the past, the Diaspora has never proven to be a reliable haven; for the Jew, the future can only be an act of faith as tenuous any other. Nor does he seem cognizant of the principle of irony which dominates Jewish history: should a day of reckoning ever come, the apostate would be buried in the same mass grave as his fellow congregants.

The Theobald-Jew will not be spared for being Theobald. For from the perspective of his enemies whom he has come mistakenly to regard as his friends, *he remains both a Jew and a traitor*, one who has betrayed his own people, and thus continues to embody the antisemitic stereotype of the Jew as untrustworthy, double-dealing and hopelessly degenerate, as one deserving of a punitive fate. It is, in fact, the fate of the native collaborator who, once he has been subverted and exploited, once he has outlived his usefulness, will be judged and condemned, sooner or later. But Theobald is not to be deterred. As the recusant who defends the Other's jaundiced vision of himself, he is delivered from the bonds of self, released from historical servitude, granted his coveted indulgence, and acquires a new identity as, let us say, Judas Centurion, the standard-bearer of militant treachery against his own people, who seeks to acquit himself in desecration. As if one could indemnify oneself against oneself. As if, to quote Horace Kallen, one could change one's grandfather.

Sometimes, of course, the motive for treachery is unabashedly crude, the desire to turn one's defencelessness to personal advantage. Such is the Jew whom Wisse anatomizes, "the ubiquitous informer, or *moser*…For every Mordecai and Esther who risked their lives to protect fellow Jews, there were schemers who turned betrayal or conversion to profit." These are the derelict Mordecais who collude with Haman, the déclassé Queen Esthers who, to quote the *Book of Esther* 9:1, labour for "the day that the enemies of the Jews hoped to have power over them."

The purchasable Jew who sells out his kinsmen, be it for lucre, confirmation, safety or esteem, represents a very old pattern of behavior. As French philosopher Shmuel Trigano writes in *Controverse numêro 10*, Jews are regularly condemned for their enemies' crimes against them, which becomes a powerful motive for treachery: In order to dodge "*la mauvaise foi planétaire,*" they switch sides, gaining temporary advantages along the way. But whether the turncoat acts from downright squalid motives or convolutedly "metaphysical" reasons, he does not see that he is the victim of a bad joke. Misconstruing parole as amnesty, our unsavoury hireling gives himself over to his own quietus. Such Jews are protected for a time by their complicity, joining the antisemitic feeding frenzy like pilot fish that clean the teeth of sharks and, as Herman Melville wrote in *The Maldive Shark*, "there find a haven when peril's abroad,/An asylum in the jaws of the Fates." But when the shark gets hungry enough, the pilot fish has been known to make a handy meal.

As I wrote in *The Big Lie*, the Jew is the Gentile's unconscious, whether it is regarded as the reservoir of destructive forces—the Id—or as the repository of unattainable ethical ideals—the Superego. In either case, the Jew is the Gentile's bad conscience. But what I did not realize when I arrived at that formulation in an attempt to explain the perdurance of antisemitism is that the Jew—or the stereotype of "the Jew"—is also, for many Jews, a central component of their own unconscious. Betrayal is thus an act of self-purgation and remission of sins. But at what cost? "When Jews lose the sense of interdependency with, and obligations of mutual responsibility toward their fellow Jews," writes Rabbi Jonathan Rosenblum, "something more than mere ethnic identity has been lost." For Rosenblum, what has been lost is "to be a member of the nation with a Divine mission." For less observant Jews, like this writer, it is the will to survive, to ensure a future for one's progeny, to counter, let us say, the "Historical mission" of nation after nation in the sordid and perennial campaign to erase a people from the face of the earth—starting with Israel.

In a paper delivered at a Brandeis University symposium on February 24, 2008, Israeli author Saul Singer stressed that the mission of the Jewish people was not mere survival but that of a higher, civilizing purpose. In a world which "lacks physical adversity and faces instead a crisis of meaning and community in the face of frayed social bonds," a world, moreover, in which Jews no longer malinger in a state of exile and dispersion, the Jewish mission becomes one of establishing social and religious coherence in the midst of anomie and torpor. There may be much truth in Singer's position; however, the world is not quite as roseate as he portrays it. For one thing, "physical adversity" is everywhere around us as is violence and upheaval. For another, Jews in the Diaspora, despite the comfort zone many inhabit, are not living in the post-exilic world of their fantasies, since a Hydra-headed antisemitism is never far from arising.

This is especially so in Europe whose ethnic composition in the coming years, Walter Laqueur soberly points out in *The Last Days of Europe*, could "lead to a new exodus of Jews from Europe. But there are not that many left, and by taking a low profile they might be able to survive in new conditions." Laqueur is obviously referring to the burgeoning Muslim population and its multicultural enablers. The key term is the troubling modal, "might," for the history of Europe is not encouraging. Under the botox, the bone structure remains the same. This is a fact that should be acknowledged and its implications absorbed. Nor, in reality, does the history of the rest of the world, whether in the Christian (or post-Christian) West beyond Europe or the Muslim East, give us much in the way of assurance. Despite the heralded benefits of assimilation, the Diaspora is by no means secure, not only for Jews complicit in the campaign against their own but for the innocent as well, those of best intention.

As Benjamin Rosendahl points out in an article for the *Jerusalem Post* (September 7, 2009) on the theme of Joseph Sus Oppenheimer (aka Jud Sus), a loyal and competent administrator who rose as court Jew to the Duke of Württemberg in 1734, only to be falsely accused of fraud, embezzlement, treason and sexual deviance, and hanged four years later, this is a collective Jewish experience: "the social rise that included its fall," and the realization "that assimilation had been in vain." The saga of Jud Sus has inspired many articles, books and plays since the mid-19th century, including the Nazi antisemitic film *Jud Sus*, but however the story is treated, it contains an important lesson for Jews: avoid complacency. Today, no matter how integrated and accepted Jews may feel in their host countries, the Diaspora is intimately involved in the fate of Israel. The bottom line is that the Diaspora needs a strong Jewish state if it is to endure. And Israel, as we know only too well, is under sustained attack on the ground, in the media, the Unions, the Churches, the NGOs, the universities, the United Nations and the political community, and may conceivably cease to exist in the not too distant future.

George Steiner wrote in *Language and Silence*, "If Israel were to be destroyed, no Jew would escape unscathed. The shock of failure, the need and harrying of those seeking refuge, would reach out to implicate even the most indifferent, the most anti-Zionist." According to Saul Bellow in *To Jerusalem and Back*, the great Israeli historian Jacob Leib Talmon was of the same mind. In a conversation with the author, Talmon feared that the destruction of Israel would bring with it the end of "corporate Jewish existence all over the world, and a catastrophe that might overtake U.S. Jewry." The fissures and schisms in the Diaspora mirror those to be found in the *Yishuv* and, in their own way, are also portentous of a grim forthcoming. Whether they know it or not, all Jews share a common journey and a common fate, as history has proven before and may well do so again. While an idealism of purpose is not to be scanted, survival remains the desideratum—the very survival that has been put in jeopardy by the negligence and discord of the Diaspora, the fickle irresponsibility of Israeli leadership like that of Ehud Olmert and Tzipi Livni and the moral defalcation of Jewish leftist intellectuals, editors and academicians in both Israel and the far abroad.

These latter constitute a family of delators who have acquired, for the time being, influence and status in the vast, anti-Zionist sodality of the Left, enjoying a negative version of what Max Weber called "lineage charisma." It seems that the wise counsel of Maimonides has no resonance for them: "All of Israel and those who are joined to it are to each other like brothers. If brother shows no compassion to brother, who will show compassion to him?"

Certainly, not his enemies.

12

Two Kingdoms?

There are moments, I must ruefully confess, when, against my better judgment and my own best interests, I too feel like giving up on the brave national experiment which is Israel, not out of resentment against my own or any sympathy with the cooked-up Palestinian narrative, but in utter stupefaction at the perpetual lack of cohesion among its citizens, its endless intestine strife at every level of civic and institutional life, the gargantuan ineptitude and systemic corruption of much of the political caste, its unwillingness to learn from history, and that portion of the country which adheres to the left-wing, secular-orthodox faith mirroring that of the sclerotic religious parties of the far right, but which is potentially far more harmful in the long term. Here the Koran is especially acute. Surah 59:14 tells us something very true about the Jews: "There is much hostility between them: their hearts are divided…"

There is a deep schism in the making, a profoundly destabilizing scenario that may yet come into play, improbable as it may seem at present. I refer to a movement simmering within Israel, in reaction to what it perceives as the left-wing sellout of the country and an administration that has collectively taken leave of its senses. This movement eerily resembles a re-enactment of the history of the Two Kingdoms of biblical times when, after the death of King Solomon, the Israelite communality broke apart into the two warring monarchies of Israel and Judah. Rehoboam and Jeroboam are once again rattling their sabres. I am very much afraid there will be an upsurge of fratricidal violence in the country, not only a war of words and clashing editorials but increased army-settler discord and the formation of Irgun-type underground. I am not referring to another *machteret*, the name applied to a 1980s right-wing terror cell, but to the growing and increasingly militant movement opposing a post-Zionist government and the leftist veer of the press, the judiciary and the many activist groups. The pipe-bomb attack on leftist professor and "peace activist" Ze'ev Sternhell on September 24, 2008 is only a portent of the future. The natural tendency of the post-Zionist Left and the mainstream press will be to denounce "Jewish extremists" of the Right, as Professor Sternhell, Ehud Olmert and others have already done. Predictably, there is no mention of the article that Sternhell published in *Haaretz* on May 11, 2001, in the midst of the terror war, supporting Palestinian violence against the settlers east of the Green Line, whom he considered natural targets. While stressing the "legitimacy of the armed resistance in the territories themselves," his advice to the terrorists was that "it would also be smart to stop planting bombs to the west of the Green Line."

In an escalating game of tit for tat, left-wing activists vandalize settlement homes, as in the alleged attack by a group of peaceniks in Shilo on October 15, 2008—one of many such instances. Olmert then announced a series of new measures against the settlers, including an increased police presence, administrative detentions and a reduction or halt to public financing. Along with the media, he accepted at face value a videotape co-produced by Palestinians and their anti-Zionist partners showing right-wing settlers brutalizing Palestinian olive-harvesters in Tel Rumeida near Hebron. He paid no attention to the fact that the videotape was carefully assessed and then rejected by the Jerusalem Magistrate's Court as an edited fabrication—something the Palestinians and the Left media are very good at, as witness the al-Durah scam. The deteriorating situation, however, must be placed in the framework of the failed policies of the Israeli government of the time, the suppression of historical truth, the folly of unilateral disengagement and the gradual drift toward capitulation to Arab and Palestinian demands, for which the Left itself is *in the main* responsible. The blame must obviously be apportioned among both sides of the divide—although I believe it needs to be acknowledged that, in the present circumstances, the hard Right is the child of the soft Left.

It is thus no passing aberration that there appears to be a growing desire, among those who regard themselves as patriots, to secede from Israel and create a new state in the ancient homeland of Judea and

Samaria, i.e., the West Bank. The rabbi-vetted attack by settlers on an IDF base in Samaria on September 10, 2008 may well presage an ever more divisive future. Shades of the pre-exilic rupture! Rabbi Shalom Dov Wolpe, founder of SOS-Israel (*Ha'Matteh L'Hatzolat Ha'am V'Ha'Aretz*), has warned: "If the government withdraws from Judea and Samaria, then we will start a new state." SOS has now embarked on a procedure to create a new flag and national anthem for the virtual state. As one observer has commented in a talkback to *The Jerusalem Post*: "As Israel arose from the ashes of the Holocaust, so a new Israel will arise from the ashes of the failed peace process"; another forecasts that "the abandoned people will have no option but to break away and form their own political entity" and that "a new state of Judah with nuclear arms and elite soldiers" will establish itself in the West Bank and the Negev by 2020.

The movement has been backed by Rabbi Dov Lior, head of the Rabbinical Council of Judea, Samaria and the Gaza Strip, who has begun to proselytize the army. Meanwhile, even more trouble is brewing over the Israeli High Court's recent decision to provide funding not only for the Orthodox but for the Reform and Conservative conversion programs as well, regarded by Orthodox Judaism as its special halachic prerogative. Sephardi Chief Rabbi Shlomo Amar, with the support of his Ashkenazi opposite number, Rabbi Yona Metzger, warned of a widening rift in the Jewish Nation (*The Jerusalem Post*, May 24, 2009).

The possibility of this "rift" has been exacerbated in the wake of the May 18, 2009 meeting between Prime Minister Benjamin Netanyahu and President Obama, resulting in the concessionary move to dismantle settler outposts in Judea and Samaria. This prompted a rabbinical call to the army to disobey orders, which in turn led Labor MK Ophir Paz-Pines to propose launching a criminal investigation against the coalition of dissident rabbis, which includes such powerful voices as Beit El Chief Rabbi Zalman Melamed, Yitzhar Rabbi David Dudkevitch, Rabbi Ya'acov Yosef who is affiliated with the Shas party and Mercaz Harav Yeshiva Rabbi Haim Steiner. Since many IDF officers and soldiers live in the settlements and outposts and are religious Zionists by conviction, the spectre of internecine dissent cannot be dismissed as a mere policy disagreement.

It is far more than that, presaging further disunity, a weakening of civic fibre and the impetus toward creating a new and independent state. Indeed, speaking before a Tel Aviv audience on January 28, 2009, Aviva Shalit, the mother of kidnapped soldier Gilad Shalit, faulted the government for abandoning her son, stating that the unwritten covenant between Israel's leaders and its soldier-citizens "has cracked." In the light of Jewish history, it would be folly to laugh off the separation scheme as merely another crank project of another splinter group that is bound to come to nothing. It has happened before and may happen again among so fissiparous a people. Clearly, such a plan and possible eventuality would create even more havoc in the region. Its *specific* outcomes, should this ever come to pass, are unforeseeable, though extremely worrying. But one thing is certain: Israel as we know it would become even more vulnerable to Arab belligerence than it presently is.

It sometimes seems as if Israel is about to unravel before our eyes, its *esprit de corps* visibly disintegrating, a country eating its seed corn as the time of famine approaches. Its governing elite of the past years was composed of people who were simply oblivious to the menace lurking in the Palestinian playbook or who claimed to be doing good but were interested only in doing well. A significant minority of its youth are intent on avoiding military service (like former Prime Minister Olmert's own sons), its intellectual *Branja* denies the validity of their own state and provides succour to the enemy, a secession movement is in process of formation with the crisis in Hebron as its epicenter, an upscale *latte* society centered in Tel Aviv wishes only to be Europeans or secular globalists, ultra-Orthodox, anti-Zionist *haredim* in the city of Beit Shemesh in the Jerusalem District terrorize non-Orthodox Anglo immigrants, wear sackcloth on Independence Day and riot over the opening of a parking lot on Shabbat. With these ultra-religious fanatics in mind, Daniel Gordis, author of *Saving Israel*, worries about "the massive fault lines running right underneath the surface of our society," which may one day erupt into open warfare. But which is worse, the anti-Zionist haredi fanatics, or the post-Zionist political wing which slipped long ago into a cataleptic stupor, routinely surrendering most of its bargaining chips at every peace conference it attends and refusing to take the necessary measures to defend the people whom it represents?

Israel, it appears, engaged in "secret" talks with Syria, putting the Golan Heights on the table. It seems obvious to me that should Israel surrender the Golan as an incentive to separate Syria from the "Iranian axis," the country will not survive. Apart from losing 15% of its water supply, Israel would find not only the Syrian military but the Iranian army and the Hizbullah militia camped on the commanding heights it has given up, leaving Israel with even less strategic depth than the little it already has. This would be the beginning of the end. Equally important to keep in mind is that Syria is governed by an Alawite dynasty, but the Alawites constitute only 11% of the Syrian population. Since the Alawites are regarded as a heretical sect by majority Sunnis, an overthrow at some future date is not out of the question, with no guarantee that an even more imprudent and bellicose regime could find itself in control of the strategic heights. According to recent surveys, 80% of Israelis oppose concessions on the Golan, yet many members of the governing political estate at the time, like Ran Cohen of the Meretz party, education minister Yuli Tamir (who introduced the study of the naqba into primary school textbooks), and of course the Kadima entourage, supported by the Left intellectual class and a compliant media, would override the wishes of the electorate.

"Among the Israeli intellectual elite," writes Melanie Phillips, "the instinct for national self-destruction reaches near-hallucinatory levels." The numberless peace movements and initiatives willing to surrender chunks of territory for nothing concrete in return are only a way of trying to metabolize chaos internally rather than facing up to it, isolating it, and keeping it at bay through determined efforts at resistance, so far as this is possible. And though Israel may be chockablock with peace movements and peace parties, all singing Kumbaya together as the pressure rises, the rockets fall and the armies mass, nothing even remotely similar is to be found in any Arab country. The Palestinian appetite for aggression remains unsated.

According to a Harry S. Truman poll conducted in March 2009, not long after the devastating Gaza war, over 54% of Palestinian respondents favour the prolongation of armed attacks against Israeli citizens.

Yet it has not occurred to the Israeli irenists that so glaring an asymmetry between the Israeli peace factions and the Palestinian/Arab incendiaries can only work against their interests. A monologue is not a dialogue, and where there is no commensurable dialogue, there can be no play. The vaunted "peace talks" are not dialogues but mismatched soliloquies, in which one side talks and cedes and the other demands and takes. The peace-mongers might do well to take the time to read the Hamas Charter where it is written that "the so-called peaceful solutions and international conferences are in contradiction to the principles of the Islamic Resistance Movement…There is no solution for the Palestinian question except through Jihad. Initiatives, proposals and international conferences are all a waste of time and vain endeavours." They may then supplement their perusal of the Charter by consulting Jean-François Revel's *How Democracies Perish.* In the minds of totalitarians, he writes, the aim of dialogue and negotiation "has never been to reach a lasting agreement but to weaken their adversary and prepare [him] to make further concessions while fostering his illusion that the new concessions…will bring stability, security, tranquility."

But whether in blindness, fatigue or weakness, Israel has for far too long chosen to ignore so perennial and timely a warning. It is as if Israel had become its own composite lost tribe, having forgotten the lesson of Jeremiah 6:13-14: "From the prophet even unto the priest every one dealeth falsely…saying peace, peace; when there is no peace." It is hard not to sympathize with the pungent remark of the Przysucha Hassidic Rebbe, Menachem Mendel of Kotzk, who said: "I could revive the dead, but I have more difficulty reviving the living." Still, I always bethink myself when I recall the ultimate futility of self-denial, or experience the undying animus against Jews and the very *real* conspiracy in the world at large against the continued existence of the Jewish state which, however mismanaged, was founded to provide a refuge for the Jewish people and to ensure their survival. The Israeli (and Jewish) experience at its most genuine is a form of historical belonging which the late Rabbi Joseph Soloveitchik, the world's leading authority on Jewish law, has defined in his philosophical reflections as "the acceptance of the past to which one is indebted and the anticipation of a future to which one is responsible"—an idea developed at length in his two seminal works, *The Lonely Man of Faith* and *The Halakhic Mind.*

This sentiment was recently echoed by Natan Sharansky in his new book *Defending Identity* where he writes that "without a feeling of connection to the generations who came before and to those who will come after, there can be enjoyment of life but not the strength to defend that life when it is endangered." Such is the commitment which the Israeli Left, a propitiating government and an indifferent citizenry may cast aside only at the peril of their disappearance. Defection is not an affordable luxury. One can only remain engaged and hope that Israel manages to resolve its internal divisions and recover its mojo before it is ushered off the stage of history. Perhaps its diplomatic losses and military embarrassments will serve to awaken it to the reality of the situation in which it finds itself, so that the famous Talmudic phrase may once again resonate: *Gam zu latovah*, "This too is for the good." Though more likely, the great sages of the Talmud, the *Tannaim*, would be stroking their beards trying to understand the nature and direction of recent Israeli policy.

Israel today, I'm afraid, needs the entire complement of *lamed vovniks*, the thirty six just men on whom, according to Jewish legend, the world's existence depends, in order merely to secure its own. How reconcile these major conflictual constituencies: the religious anti-Zionist *Haredim*, the secular post-Zionist lefties, the religious Zionist patriots living in the settlements and the secular Zionist mainstream opposed to all three of the former groupings? Israelis must show that they actually deserve a state.

Perhaps the results of the 2009 election, which returned Benjamin Netanyahu and a Likud administration to power, will prove to be a step in the right direction, despite the pressure of the current American administration and European governments on Israel to make ever more unproductive concessions to world opinion and a crafty "negotiating partner." An encouraging sign indicating that Netanyahu may have the "right stuff" is that Abbas has balked at returning to the negotiating table, hoping that pressure from the Obama administration "will gradually force Netanyahu out of office" (*Washington Post*, May 29, 2009). A Prime Minister who rattles the Palestinians rather than one who caters to them and to their unrealistic demands is, at the very least, a favourable augury.

David Ben-Gurion once said, "Only those who believe in miracles are realists in the Middle East." Whether or not we believe in miracles, let us at least be realists.

13

Bleeding History

At the same time as Jew sets his teeth against Jew, the drama of internecine strife within the faith-community itself, whatever manifestation it may assume, does not for a moment absolve the Gentile/Islamic world of its fierce and agelong oppression of the Jewish people, scattered, contentious and divided as it may be. Certainly, little has changed in the Middle East. On the eve of the 1967 war, Egyptian Radio's "Voice of the Arabs" called for a war of "extermination of Zionist existence"; today the Iranian President threatens to "wipe Israel off the map" in a "single storm." Former revisionist historian Benny Morris, who seems to have undergone a political awakening, takes us back to the 1948 War of Independence as the starting point of the ceaseless Islamic campaign against the existence of a Jewish state. In his *1948: A History of the First Arab-Israeli War*, Morris argues that 1948 was only the first battle in what is nothing less than a Muslim-inspired holy war and a zero-sum game that will neutralize all efforts at negotiating a genuine peace. His latest offering, *One State, Two States*, goes even further in the direction of *real* history and rehabilitating the Jewish state.

But the ultimate source of Islamic Jew-hatred goes back to the Koran itself. Anyone who doubts this need only read it, and linger over such surahs as 1:7, 2:61, 3:112, 4:47, 4:60, 5:60, 5:78, 7:166, 9:29, 58:14, 98:7, to mention only the most obvious. There are, it is true, a sprinkling of passages which seem to associate Jews with the "Land of Promise" (e.g., 5:21, 10:93-94), but only one, 17:104, presumably allows the Israelites to dwell there, although only for a time. This latter passage is disputed by Islamic commentators who debate whether the lease given by Allah to the Jews extends to the Day of Judgment or only to the rejection of Jesus and the destruction of the Second Temple. Meanwhile, the pestilential atmosphere now pervading the Islamic realm, the Western democracies and the Third World only reinforces the sense and possibility of impending calamity—the latest installment in the chronicle of Jewish vulnerability. The political and intellectual climate we have created has become so lopsided and surreal that, should Islamic terrorists ever succeed in exploding a nuclear bomb in a Western city, the International community would probably urge retaliatory action against Israel.

The Jew bleeds history, the favoured victim of a hematophagous world. Although there seems to be a certain inevitability at work in this historical process, spreading unchecked like a massive infestation of webworm, there is not and there never has been any moral justification for antisemitism, and those who persist in harbouring such morbific sentiments, whether on the level of the individual, the *vox populi* or the body politic, are guilty of a crime against humanity—precisely as was the United Nations when in 1975 it passed its infamous Resolution 3379 declaring Zionism a "racist and imperialist ideology" and "a threat to world peace and security." Although Resolution 4686 repealed its predecessor in 1991, the stigma remains and the locution "Zionism is racism" concludes many of the votes of UN agencies.[14] In point of fact, the "Zionism is racism" platform is really a mobius strip of self-implication, twisting around on itself to become a racist ideology of its own, targeting a particular ethnic and national community—one that has been the victim of apartheid practices from time immemorial to the present—for unnuanced and aprioristic condemnation. Thus, to take one example from a veritable jubilee, the UN Human Rights Council's fact-finding mission into the shelling of Beit Hanoun in Gaza began its resolution by accusing Israel of the "wilful killing of Palestinian civilians" *even before embarking on its investigation.*

The same perversion applies to the growing cohort of prejudicial voices who decry the alleged Jewish influence on the world media—which are, as it happens, distinctly anti-Israeli and anti-Zionist—and on the course of American politics, which, with respect to the powerful State Department, is and has long been clearly unfavourable to Israel's welfare. In late 19th century France, we had the "Jewish Syndicate." In the 1930s in the United States and Britain, there was a pervasive belief in the "Jewish conspiracy." Today, as we have seen, it's called the "Jewish Lobby."[15] The strategy of disendowment remains the same. And so may the result. In a speech given to the Domestic Affairs Committee of the German Bundestag in June 2008, journalist Henryk Broder differentiated between the classical antisemite and the modern antisemite. The latter, he said, "does not have a shaved head. He has good manners and often an academic title as well…The modern anti-semite does not believe the *Protocols of the Elders of Zion*. But instead he fantasizes about an 'Israel lobby' that is supposed to control American foreign policy like a tail that wags the dog." Broder concluded his talk by urging the elite group of politicians and academics in the audience to devote their attention "to the modern anti-Semitism that wears the disguise of anti-Zionism and to its representatives. You will find some of the latter among your own ranks."

Of course, there is little public recognition of the fact that it is only natural for Diaspora groups to seek to influence foreign policy in their adoptive countries. Immigrant communities from Poland, Armenia, Greece, Pakistan, Mexico, India and now from the Arab countries have all successfully campaigned in support of their homelands, going so far as to affect congressional elections in the United States. This is only customary professional conduct and is no different for Jewish organizations. But such activities do not justify accusing the latter of working through a powerful and iniquitous lobby that is somehow in a class of its own, an imputation which is an obvious distortion of a practice common to many if not most immigrant Diasporas. And not only such expatriate groups. There are in excess of 30,000 lobbyists on Capitol Hill. According to *The Guardian/Observer* website (January 8, 2006), Big Pharma is the major lobbyist; and, as should be common knowledge, the Farm Lobby and Midwest agrabusiness is not far behind. These are the real untouchables. The American Israel Public Affairs Committee (AIPAC) is a well-organized advocacy group with some clout on the Hill but it is by no means the behemoth its critics have made it out to be. And like any other of the thousands of such associations, it has every legal right to try and make its presence felt. The only problem is that it is pro-Israel—as it should be. Its function is the reason for its existence, *which is the case for every other advocacy group with an agenda, whether political or fiscal.* To isolate AIPAC as a conspiratorial entity, as distinct in its means, subversive in its impact and treasonable in its policies is both false and slanderous, another antisemitic canard titivating as public concern.

Clearly, Israel is at war on many fronts, apart from the *physical* threat to its very existence—and not only its own. Indeed, Israel is like the West's unappreciated sniffer dog: it locates the weapons caches and shipments and nuclear installations in the region and is then returned to the kennels on short rations. Which leaves it no choice but to break free and complete the job its "handlers" have thus far failed to carry out. Just as conspicuously, the many boycott and divestment schemes of the Churches, the trade unions and the pension funds are really a form of *economic* warfare against the country—the contemporary version of *Kristallnacht* which hurls market enactments through the windows of Israeli trade and commerce. The travesty about the "Jewish Lobby," promoted by a growing number of "liberal" writers and professors and boiling over into the general public, is an avatar of the *political* warfare being waged against Israel. The "Zionism is racism" bogey is only the latest form that the *ideological* warfare against the Jewish state has taken.[16]

As Josephus writes in *Against Apion*, "unspeakable mischiefs have been occasioned by such calumnies as have been raised against us." What we are observing is a new and reinvigorated Inquisition percolating across the entire globe. Its proponents and enablers proclaim their righteousness in attacking what they consider to be a fallen state, and large segments of the public that unthinkingly accept this twisted narrative are unaware that they have been misled and abused—it is, so to speak, part of the informatic atmosphere. This is how the new century begins, but how different is it, really, from the beginning of the last century with Vienna mayor Karl Lueger's publicized movement for boycotting Jews? We have seen what that stirring call to anti-Jewish action led to. There is a strict rule operating here: demonization inevitably precedes disaster.

Alain Finkielkraut in *The Imaginary Jew* has made a similar point with regard to the way in which the cowcatcher term "Zionism" is used to pillory Jews and the Jewish state and devise the means of their exclusion from the normative. "All that's required to transform the entire community into a secret society is to subsume all these differences under a single name: Zionism." For the designation and concept of Zionism as deployed by the antisemite "cancels all nuances, suppresses distinctions, and abolishes differences of degree." And Zionism, naturally, means Israel. The upshot is that "Terrorism is a direct consequence of this distortion [since] there are no longer any innocents, only a 'Zionist entity.' " The "many" have been codified as the "one." As a result, says Finkielkraut, "it's the Jew alone (or, after Auschwitz, the Zionist) who fits the bill as the Grand Enemy." And the political condensation of the category "Jew" is the state of Israel.

The issue is further ravelled by the European impetus toward a transnational authority that seeks to overcome the presumed limitations of the nation-state in a globalizing world. The Benelux seed has blossomed into a post-Edenic garden of unsustainable welfarism and of merged—and therefore vague—identities presided over by an all-controlling administrative deity, with predictably unfolding results. For in this world Paradise is not an option. The quest for political transcendence can lead only to eventual banishment from the imagined garden and to the flaming sword which turns every way. History has shown that when the paradigm of the City of God is imposed without humility or nuance upon the Earthly City, in whatever imperial modification that beau ideal may assume, or when the earthly city replaces in its self-sufficiency the heavenly city, some sort of political deformation invariably ensues.

The Babelian hybris of the project is evident in the overheated rhetoric of Antonio Negri's and Michael Hardt's jargon-clotted, academic bestseller, *Empire*, a reblocked version of an old hat theory of human emancipation. "The mythology of the languages of the multitude," the duo write, "interprets the telos of the earthly city, torn away by the power of its own destiny from any belonging or subjection to a city of God, which has lost all honor and legitimacy." The revolutionary violence these authors promote has been tried before in the social gulag of the Communist *urbs proletariorum*, leading to the suffering, disempowerment and impoverishment of hundreds of millions. While the EU (both the people and their administrators) obviously does not qualify as part of the "multitude" of the dispossessed, eulogized by the authors as "constellations of powerful singularities" that constitute a "radical counterpower," and while the EU power structure certainly does not envision the military oppression of its own citizens in order to impose a policy of social and economic egalitarianism, it is, despite its apparent reality, no less of a political figment. The state of civic and cultural beatitude envisioned by the EU cannot stand up indefinitely against the rigors and pressures of unforgiving reality or the staying power of felt nationality. Ironically, the proof sits in its own frontyard, like a particularly unsightly garden gnome. Belgium, the bureaucratic center of the EU, is currently in the throes of a potential breakup, threatening to split into two new nation states, one serving the French-speaking Walloons and the other the Dutch-speaking Flemings. Even the leftish *Economist* has suggested that "a praline divorce is in order" (September 6, 2007). In the interim, as Natan Sharansky argues in *Defending Identity*, the diminution of the sense of national identity under the aegis of a post-identity ideology makes Europe helpless to fend off the threat posed by its growing Muslim population whose own sense of identity is strong and self-assured.

Should the Tranzis—a term coined by blogger David Carr and expanded by the Hudson Institute's John Fonte as "transnational progressives"— eventually win the day, the political postlude would be unnerving. Transnational progressivism may be non-violent but it is demonstrably coercive in its plan to transfer power from elected representation to an unaccountable bureaucracy, specifically, to a commissariat of self-declared progressives who know what is best for the people. In fact, the consortium of EU bureaucrats has come disturbingly to resemble Iran's Guardian Council, an unelected body of clerics and experts on Islamic law, whose decisions are inviolable. Indeed, the tag "progressive," adopted by both socialist parties and cosmocrat organizations, has now become a synonym for its antonym, "regressive."

In a closely reasoned article for *The Chronicle of Higher Education* (August 9, 2007), Gadi Taub has cogently argued that the European valorization of "institutions that transcend the nation-state" is, in essence, "a liberal assault on nationalism [that] is beginning to look like an assault on the principle of government without the consent of the governed," since such institutions "exercise great influence, even jurisdiction, over people and peoples who have little or no democratic control over them." In this way, untutored liberalism (or post-liberalism) threatens to become a new kind of tyranny and this tyranny recognizes both the United States and Israel, which are constitutional democratic orders, as obstacles to its hegemonic blueprint for what Fonte calls "post-constitutional supranational governance." This is the malware lodged in the European hard drive. It is almost a law of human behaviour that a small, unelected group invested with immense powers will not act in the interests of the mass of the people for any length of time. *Quis custodiet ipsos custodes*? asked the Roman poet Juvenal. Who will watch the watchmen?

The United States, despite the backsliding of the Democratic party from its Scoop Jackson legacy and the policy meltdown under the Obama administration, widespread academic dissidence, the vast number of bluenecks seeking peace in our time and the activities of a vermicular press, is certainly in a better position than Israel, if only because its power is still immense and it is not under daily attack by a circumambient enemy. Many who spend their time or earn their livings reviling America must surely intuit that the object of their detestation can absorb their rant and prattle and that America will not conveniently disappear tomorrow or the day after—even though its time may be coming. They are still free to ply their disreputable trade.

Moreover, though few are ready to candidly admit the truth, most are at least subliminally aware that America is *needed* by the world, whether as the chief donor to the United Nations, or for its munificent charity and aid to other countries—America outcontributes any other nation in AIDS relief for Africa as it did for Tsunami-ravaged East Asia—or, despite its current troubles, as the lynchpin of the world economy, or as a potential bulwark against destabilizing military threats wherever they may arise. America's greatest enemy is not an external foe but its own developing fault lines. The tectonic plates that undergird the sense of national unity may be moving apart, but its collapse is not yet imminent and its presence as a world force remains indispensable. Robert Kagan in *The Return of History* points to the "rise of great power competition and the clashing interests and ambitions across Eurasia" which makes "the umbrella of American predominance" necessary to prevent total instability in the region.

Israel, however, is not felt as needed in any way although, as previously mentioned, the world would be much poorer in the fields of cybernetics, medicine, alternative energy and agriculture without it. Quite the contrary, Israel is perceived as a gadfly and a stubborn nettle, a perpetual irritant and provocation. Treated as an anomaly, a misfortune, a historical vestige, a pariah, a dispensable construct or a political retrogression, it is nevertheless a nation that up to now has tenaciously fought for its existence rather than acquiesce in its disappearance or subsumption into an authoritarian, all-embracing, superordinate, administrative organism, let alone a regional confederacy. I say "up to now," for Israel's left-wing and post-Zionist Jews are diligently working to undermine the Jewish identity of the nation in a disastrous attempt to turn it into a kind of mini-Europe. Canadian historian Ramsay Cook, who considers nationalism a "reactionary ideology," long ago understood the significance of the Zionist experience for the modern world. In his 1965 essay, "The Historian and Nationalism," he writes: "It is no accident that the first Western people with a historical consciousness is also the people whose history provides the archetypes of modern nationalism: the Jewish people." The internationalist Left today, in its castigation of nationalism as an organizing principle of political life, has strongly endorsed this position, even though it is domiciled far more in elaborate theory than in beneficial practice.

It is also split by a contradiction, for the European Union and the transnational Left are strongly committed to the creation of a Palestinian state which will one day claim territorial inviolability and strive to assert both its national and theological character. But Zionism is a different matter altogether. As Mark Lilla suggested in a *New Republic* essay, in European eyes the Zionist enterprise represents "a political atavism that enlightened Europeans should spurn." He is alert to the resident irony. "Once upon a time, the Jews were mocked for not having a nation-state. Now they are criticized for having one." Finkielkraut arrived at the same *compte-rendu*. Writing in *Azure* (No.

18, 2004), he asserts: "Instead of accusing these inveterate nomads of conspiring to bring about the deracination of Europe, we now charge these latecomers to autochthony with falling into that very state which characterized the Europeans before remorse…compelled them to put universal principles above territorial sovereignty." How fossil-like, refractory and unEuropean is the Jewish state! How resistant to progressive thought and a better future for all men and women of good will! A Palestinian state, however, is fine and dandy, regardless of its vestigial nature. In this case, transnationalism is trumped by anti-Zionism. It should come as no surprise that, despite the fact that Hamas is a designated terrorist organization, Kyriacos Triantaphyllides, head of an EU parliamentary delegation to Gaza on November 3, 2008, issued an invitation to Hamas "legislators" to visit EU headquarters in Brussels.

And yet the European (as well as the Western in general, and Arab) insistence on the creation of a Palestinian state and the preoccupation with the Palestinian cause are, at bottom, duplicitous. This should be obvious when we consider the European (as well as the Western in general, and Arab) response—or rather, *lack of response*—to the Iranian threat to visit nuclear annihilation upon Israel. For if Israel should be destroyed in a nuclear attack, Gaza, the West Bank and one million Israeli-Palestinians would also be annihilated. Physical destruction, radiation poisoning and total economic collapse would eliminate Palestinian Arabs as effectively as it would Israeli Jews. Yet this horrendous consequence is never considered and certainly never mentioned whenever Ayatollah Rafsanjani or President Ahmadinejad issue their chilling calls to nuclear holocaust—inarguable proof that the real agenda in play is not to liberate Palestine but to liquidate Israel. In failing to recognize or care about the fate of the Palestinians under such apocalyptic conditions, it becomes evident that the noisy and righteous concern with Palestinian welfare is merely a covert operation to ensure the disappearance of Israel, whether violently, politically or demographically. In the final analysis, so long as Israel can be rendered desolate, the Palestinians can go hang.

If the West had any sense—something we frankly cannot expect of the Arab world—it would recognize Israel as a positive addition to the family of nations, a nation whose rebirth has something of the unprecedented, even the miraculous, about it. Israel is the first country in the world whose scientific/medical establishment has successfully managed, through pre-implantation genetic diagnosis and in-vitro fertilization, to produce a normal baby from a dwarf mother. It is hard to resist a political analogy with Zionism, a heteroclite movement almost universally derided, and its offspring, Israel, which is, for all its problems and by any sane comparison with its Arab neighbours, a healthy and vigorous country in a part of the world that has been ailing for centuries. The medical marvel only recapitulates the political unprecedentedness which the Jewish state embodies. But because Israel has had the audacity to survive and grow in the face of unmitigated Arab ferocity and relentless international reprobation, because it has shown the world what a despised and isolated people could do by maintaining faith in itself and adhering to principle—at least until recently—it has reaped the undying hostility of the bulk of mankind. Whatever admiration its nigh-miraculous birth and development may have earned the country, it is mainly of the grudging kind.

Those who would seek to reverse this trend are faced with a nearly insurmountable task: speaking out on behalf of Israel has become the third rail of contemporary political discourse. And there is no reprieve in sight. Could we take a step back for the sake of triangulation and look at the matter objectively, we might actually be startled at what we are seeing. Why this lurid and tumescent preoccupation with Israel on the part of millions of people worldwide who have absolutely no stake in the country's affairs and a throng of nations that have no practical interest in the political issues involved? The baleful and unwavering focus by countless individuals, social groups, professional societies, political parties, media outlets, educational institutions, blogs, websites, NGOs and national governments on what, for the most part, is really not their business and to which no other nation on the planet has been even remotely subjected, including the most reprehensible violators of civil rights and of commonly accepted norms of conduct, can be explained in only one way. The Jew must be made to pay for what the world does—that's the drill.

One does not see Israel sending its emissaries to Paris to advise the French on their problem with rioting Muslim immigrants in that country's self-designated "Sensitive Urban Zones"; or dispatching official representatives to Washington to urge the Americans to regulate their border problems with Mexican illegals and instructing the President where these refugees are not permitted to settle; or flying in a military delegation to Moscow to chide the Russians for their demolition of Grozny and their repeat performance in Georgia; or addressing stern reprimands to the Chinese for repressing the people of Tibet, submitting the Falun Gong to organ harvesting and incarcerating dissidents; or counselling the Canadians to return vast tracts of territory to their original inhabitants, who have a far stronger case than the Palestinians, and then granting sovereignty to the restive province of Quebec; or sanctimoniously intervening in the British mismanagement of their internal affairs and demanding that the Jewish *Bet Din* receive the same official sanction and power as the Shari'a courts.

Whenever Israel is the topic, there is a kind of prurient glee in diminishing it, a slavering pornography of the spirit that delights in rendering it naked and vulnerable. The reaction Israel provokes is almost Pavlovian in its predictability: let the Israeli bell sound, the saliva begins to spurt. This is what History professor Gil Troy of McGill University calls "Zionophobia," which he defines as "the irrational hatred of Israel and Jewish nationalism." Zionophobia masks "antisemitism by demonizing Israel in the guise of defending the downtrodden," which accounts for the poster boy status of the Palestinians. "Surprisingly," he continues on his blog site, "this anti-modern, anti-democratic, deeply illiberal ideology has influenced academics, intellectuals, NGO-activists, and United Nations bureaucrats who believe they champion modernity, universalism and human rights." Well, perhaps not so "surprisingly."

Israel, let us remember, is the collective incarnation of the Jew *qua* Jew, but since it is also a national state, this enables the deft and sinuous Jew-hater to escape moral censure under the sign of "impartial" criticism of an independent nation. And the criticism remains as grotesque as it is interminable. Thus when Israel targeted rocket crews in Gaza after a particularly heavy barrage on its Negev communities, Mahmoud Abbas as usual cried "massacre." When the IDF killed four terrorists in the West Bank, including the mastermind of the attack which murdered the eight Talmudic students in Jerusalem, Abbas shouted "ethnic cleansing." When Islamic Jihad, with the tacit approval of Hamas, renewed its Kassam attacks against Israel even during the an acknowledged ceasefire, journalist Adam Entous placed the blame on an Israeli *retaliatory* raid—"deadly" was his choice descriptor. The Israeli strike "prompted militants"—not terrorists, militants—"to step up rocket attacks, most of which cause no injuries and little damage" (*Reuters*, December 22, 2008). The damage, however, is substantial and the *Reuters* stooge did not see fit to mention those who had been killed, maimed and traumatized in these attacks. A few days after his article appeared, another Israeli was killed and five residents of the Negev city of Netivot hospitalized.

And when Israel briefly reduced diesel fuel deliveries to Gaza in response to another torrent of Kassams on Sderot, as many as fifty in one day, it was predictably denounced by UNRWA, and by practically every NGO that meddles in the area, for creating a "humanitarian crisis." There is no reference to the fact that the direct result of Israel's disengagement from Gaza was the *quadrupling* of rocket and mortar strikes on the country's southwestern flank. There is, of course, nothing resembling a "humanitarian crisis" in those Israeli towns and kibbutzes that have been under attack since the disengagement and indeed for the last seven years and where normal life has ground to a halt and the economy has tanked. There is—who can deny it?—no "humanitarian crisis" in Sderot where recent studies have shown that three quarters of its children between the ages of 7 and 12 suffer from post-traumatic stress disorder, where the warning sirens sounded on average every two hours, and where half the businesses and a substantial percentage of the population have had to relocate.

Nor were any of these altruistic organizations interested in stating the obvious: *Israel is under no obligation to lend its support to its self-avowed enemy*, providing Gaza—whose population elected Hamas by a wide margin and supports terror attacks against Israel by an even wider margin—with medical treatment, diesel fuel, electrical power and food shipments. As we have noted, the Geneva Conventions do not apply in this situation since Gaza can no longer credibly be described as "occupied." So we need to ask. What other nation in the world heals and victuals its enemies or allows its own population centers to undergo relentless bombardment? Would the United States, for example, have remained quiescent for a single day in the face of incessant Mexican rocket attacks on El Paso? Would it go on serving its attackers' energy needs? Would it continue jauntily to supply Mexico's wants and necessities?

The situation is so absurd and self-defeating as to defy belief. Ashkelon generates 75% of Gaza's electricity supply, yet territories within the Ashekelon Regional Council have been the object of over 800 rockets fired from the Strip, one of which may some day strike the very generator that provides the electricity the Gazans need and the world community has insisted on. This self-destructive policy was in operation again when, on April 9, 2008, Gaza terrorists killed two Israeli civilians at the Nahal Oz fuel depot that transferred fuel shipments to the Gaza Generating Company power plant—unless, of course, this was merely another cynical ploy on the part of Hamas to force Israel to close the depot and thereby incite the "international community" and the ever-compliant United Nations to protest Israel's presumed cruelty and barbarism. When the Nahal Oz and Karni crossings came under a renewed Hamas mortar barrage on May 4, forcing fuel and food trucks to turn back, Hamas immediately complained about shortages and UN officials, who had to cancel supply deliveries, refused to implicate the terrorist regime.

The many "well-intentioned" peace outfits and most of the world's governments have not seen fit to recognize the plain reality of the overall situation. Once the incessant rocket attacks on Israeli civilians should be stopped, targeted assassinations would cease and medical access, food, fuel and power shipments would flow freely—although, and it is important to emphasize the point, *Israel would still be under no obligation whatsoever to cater to or initiate relations with another state or people*. Such is the rule the Muslim nations have adopted wholesale vis à vis Israel. It is the justification—however misbegotten since not submitted to a plenary vote of all its affiliates and members—behind the divestment campaigns of the Churches, NGOs, universities and trade unions, and, indeed, it is an axiom the "world community" has sanctioned for its own members, with the hypocritical exception of the Jewish state. This is a basic principle of the *jus gentium*: there is no legal compulsion for a competent authority to "do business" with or provide succour to those it does not wish to. Nevertheless, from the unreflected perspective of the rest of the world, Israel, which owes nothing to Gaza, must continue to furnish its adversaries with their stipulated requirements. Of course, there is also a basic principle of moral honesty that should be acknowledged: There is no ethical justification for boycotting a nation while continuing to accept the many benefits that flow from it; in Israel's case, its technological, medical and agricultural contributions to mankind.

It is now known that the electricity "blackout" in Gaza was staged by Hamas, which, while continuing to receive its normal quota from the Ashkelon generator, shut down its central power station and invited journalists to commiserate, including al-Jazeera which was Johnny-on-the-spot to film the "spontaneous" candlelight vigil orchestrated by Hamas and blamed on Israel. Hamas is adept at putting the old Turkish saying into practice: "The clever thief has the master of the house hanged." (This *fabricated* crisis was reported by a mere handful of news outlets, such as *HonestReporting.com* and, *mirabile dictu*, as documented by Khaled Abu Toameh, by several Palestinian journalists who noted that Gaza Prime Minister Ismail Haniyeh and his colleagues were sitting in a curtained room around a table with burning candles—in broad daylight!) Scarcely a day goes by in which Israel is not condemned for acting *as any other nation would act* under similar circumstances—except that Israel rarely does, usually choosing restraint over response. But the germ of the issue is that such anti-Zionist posturing is not politically motivated; it is nothing more than the drapery which cloaks a far deeper and more insidious agenda. And despite our seemingly principled disclaimers, we know what it is.

A thought experiment is appropriate here. Can we imagine what the official and media response would be if Israeli vigilantes were daily firing rockets into Beit Hanun in northern Gaza or if the IDF crossed the border into Lebanon to kill and kidnap Hizbullah operatives as a matter of policy? Let us carry our thought experiment a little further. Can we conceive what the public outcry would have been if the 9/11, 7/7 and Madrid bombers had been *Jewish*? If Jews had gone on a killing spree in Mumbai? There would have been no attempt to dispatch government officials to reassure the Jewish community lest it be "offended." There would have been no striking of deliberative committees involving members of the Rabbinate to suggest ways of defusing the crisis, or a profusion of editorials in most of the leading newspapers forcefully insisting on the peaceful nature of the nation's Jewish citizenry, or Church councils advocating the adoption of certain legal tractates from the Talmud and promoting interfaith dialogue to show their comradely sensitivity, or teams of intellectual pundits arguing that these Jewish terrorists had a legitimate grievance which must be redressed, or university faculties convening to denounce America and the Arabs for creating the situation which led Jews to react as they did, or trade unions passing resolutions to boycott Arab oil. Would the American Administration have elevated Abraham Foxman of the Anti-Defamation League to the U.S. Commission on International Religious Freedom, as it did Talal Eid, an imam with close ties to the Saudi-controlled Muslim World League and a proponent of shari'a courts? Would London ex-mayor Ken Livingstone have welcomed Rabbi Ovadia Yosef, former Sephardic chief rabbi of Israel and spiritual leader of the orthodox Shas party, as an honoured guest rather than Yusuf al-Qaradawi, spiritual leader of the Muslim Brotherhood? Would Spanish PM Zapatero have donned a kippa for the cameras during the Hizbullah/Israel war rather than a keffiyeh? Would the Belgian government have ordered that kosher food be served in the schools in Antwerp?

Can anyone honestly doubt that the opposite would have been the case? The Jewish community would have been ostracized and attacked as recidivist, archaic and violence-prone. It would have been condemned for undermining the foundations of civic life. It would have been branded in many quarters as an enemy of the state. It would have been subject to a media pogrom. It would have been regarded with suspicion in almost every walk of life. It would have been proscribed by the more visceral antisemites as aspiring to world domination, as per *The Protocols of the Elders of Zion*, which would enjoy increased sales around the globe. Can anyone realistically believe it would have been coddled, soothed and extenuated as was the Muslim community in the aftermath of Islamic terror? Indeed, the stirrings in the current historical crucible would make this impossible since antisemitism is an important factor in the rise of Islamophilia. What K.S. Pinson wrote in his 1954 study *Modern Germany*—"Anti-semitism as an old, deeply-rooted and ubiquitous phenomenon in the Western world could serve better than anything else to galvanise and diffuse pro-Nazi sentiment throughout the world"—would apply today to the spread of pro-Islamic sentiment.

It is time to face the truth. The *reasons* for antisemitism are no doubt multifarious, but the major *cause* of antisemitism is that Jews happen to draw breath. In the speech mentioned earlier, Henryk Broder distinguished between a prejudice and a resentment: "a prejudice concerns a person's behavior; a resentment concerns that person's very existence. Anti-semitism is a resentment. The anti-Semite does not begrudge the Jew how he is or what he does, but that he is at all. The anti-Semite takes offense as much at the Jew's attempts to assimilate as at his self-marginalization. Rich Jews are exploiters; poor Jews are freeloaders....The anti-Semite blames Jews for everything and its opposite." Broder hits it on the nose, as it were. If the early Zionists with (temporary) British agreement in principle had settled in a part of Uganda as a substitute homeland, or had improbably found a *pied à terre* in Angola or Cyrenaica (Libya), or had followed through on the Galveston scheme of 1907-1914, or if the 1928 Soviet proposal to create a Jewish socialist republic in Birobidzhan in eastern Siberia where Jews would function under their own institutions had not turned out to be a fraud, or if Israelis could be teleported to Alaska to please Mahmoud Ahmadinejad and as novelist Michael Chabon imagined, antisemites would still have found something to resent and execrate and antisemitism would have continued unabated.

Is it not revealing that antisemitism appears even in countries that are virtually empty of Jews? Mahmoud Ahmadinejad blaming Israel and the Jews for rising food prices across the globe and Muammar Gaddafi accusing Israel and the Jews for the Darfur crisis are only the tired old rhetoric of the Muslim world. There are only 25,000 Jews in Iran and, at last count, none in Libya. The anomaly lies elsewhere.

Soeren Kern, whom we have met above, considers Spain the most antisemitic country in Europe, nearly half of its people harboring negative opinions of Jews. Yet the Jewish community in Spain is infinitesmal, with only 12,000 Jews out of a population of 42 million, less than .05% (*Pajamas Media*, December 30, 2008). Similarly, there are only 1,300 Jews in Norway, approximately .003% out of a population of 4,645,000 million, yet Norway is the major Scandinavian purveyor of anti-Zionist and antisemitic attitudes and beliefs, and indeed challenges Spain for the European honor (*Behind the Humanitarian Mask*, Manfred Gerstenfeld, ed.) One remembers the graffiti in Potsdam after German reunification: *Juden Raus*, "Jews Out." There were no Jews in Potsdam. (As of this writing, Britain seems to have leaped into the forefront of the European antisemitic hatefest, with France and Sweden breathing down its neck.)

Then there is Japan, a world-leader in the promulgation of antisemitic material though one would have to search far and wide to find a Jew in that country. Many writers, publishers and organizations in Japan are preoccupied with *Yudakaya*, "the Jewish peril." According to the Stephen Roth Institute, books like *The Protocols of the Elders of Zion*, *The International Jew* and *Mein Kampf* are regularly reprinted in new editions. Authors such as Masami Uno, who runs two institutes on the Jewish peril, Ryu Ota, the publisher of the journal *Mantra* and author of *The Jewish Plan for the Occupation of Japan* (yes, dear reader, you read this right), Yakobu Morana, author of *The Last Warning from the Devil/The Jews* and Eisuke Sasagawa whose *The Devil's Warning* blames the Jews for AIDS, cancer and Alzheimer's produce works that vie in popularity with the propaganda spread by left-wing journalists like Ryuichi Hirokawa and university professors like Yuzo Itagaki, who writes about "the Nazi character of Zionism." "Cheap, soft-core literature on 'Jewish omnipotence' in business and in general," says Roth, "as well as hard-core anti-Semitic propaganda, sell well in Japan. Fascination caused by ignorance, but also in some cases fear and hatred of Jews, probably explain the great popularity of both types of anti-Semitic *yudayamono* (Jewish books)." Indeed, Jew-hatred is the one issue on which the Japanese Left and Right are united.

The Spanish, Norwegian and Japanese examples, bizarre as they may seem, are only an illustration of a worldwide phenomenon. Antisemitism is here to stay. This is because antisemitism is unlike other forms of irrational hatred and operates under a different set of laws. One might put it this way: *because it has happened before, it will happen again*, which is not the tautology or unverifiable assumption that it appears to be. We need to recognize the mechanics that operate in this past-future homology. Antisemitic sentiments, outbreaks, pogroms and holocausts, in virtue of their *millennial repeatability*, have become entrenched in human consciousness as a "natural" inevitability, as something that *must* happen again because it has *consistently* happened before. Antisemitism and its consequences as they act themselves out in the social and historical realms have gradually come to acquire the character of a deeply harboured expectation, a necessary effect of an immutable cause, as if it were a part of the phenomenal world, the prolonged absence of which dimly registers as a gap in the normal sequence of events. This gap or hiatus must be filled to restore the equilibrium of things, which is why antisemitism is felt as somehow legitimate. It is its recession that is intuited as unnatural.

The subsidence of antisemitism for an extended period is tantamount to the moon undergoing a protracted eclipse: something is wrong in the natural order, producing uncertainty and apprehension and requiring that the balance of nature be restored and reaffirmed. The moon has its familiar cycles because, according to the laws of the physical world, it must have them; an eclipse is a rare and temporary event. Antisemitism, too, will have its eclipses, but they are necessarily ephemeral. The primordial hatred of which we are speaking will continue to circle and shine and proceed through its phases because, whatever may have given it its original impetus, *it has always done so—and therefore it always will*. True, a brief obscuring of this lunatic radiation may also be regarded as an aspect of natural process, but it is its brevity rather than its occurrence that is considered natural and which renders it acceptable.

Hatred of the Jew has come to be understood across the great wave of time as a function of how the world works and, therefore, of how the world is supposed to work. The colloquial mind thinks: *it has gone on for so long, there must be something to it*. This constitutes its justification—an irrational hatred masking as a rational presumption. It is something that has occurred so often in the past, and has kept on happening wherever Jews have settled, that it is perceived in the depths of the psyche to have moved from the dimension of history over into the structure of nature. It is as if antisemitism has now become part of our synaptic equipment, which is why it will persist until the last Jew.

The profound anxiety and sense of desolation that Jean Améry (aka Hans Meyer) records in *At The Mind's Limits* is real and ineluctable. This is a world, he declares, "whose still unresolved death sentence I acknowledge as a social reality." Let no Gentile justifier or temporizing Jew take false comfort in mere denial, self-delusion, the bromides of pliable rhetoric or the seductions of sweet reason. The Jew must remain alert, always ready to defend himself, and never submit to an unfounded belief in some eventual bucolic resolution—in this sense, the past is larger than the future. And the proof is all around us in the present.

The Jewish community is now under prolonged attack from many different quarters and in many different ways, from suicide attacks and missile camisades in Israel to murderous strikes in other parts of the world to the mounting of conspiracy theories in the blogosphere to the numberless tractarian screeds flooding the marketplace to unfriendly newspaper editorials to "learned" columns and papers condemning the malefic "Jewish lobby" to campaigns of boycott and divestment emanating from major Western institutions to United Nations resolutions and NGO reports to Durban-type conferences to howls of "massacre" whenever Israel moves to defend itself against its enemies. (One remembers the hue and cry of massacre in Jenin, where the real massacre was of 23 young Israeli soldiers who might still be alive had Israel not tried to avoid civilian casualties and attacked the terrorist nest from the air.) Add to this the spate of Islamic sermons promising the eradication of the Jewish people from the face of the earth and the imminent nuclear threat of the Iranian leadership—and then let us convince ourselves that nothing out of the ordinary is happening.

National officials, press barons, journalists, public intellectuals and a growing segment of ordinary people are tapping deep into the poisoned aquifer of anti-Jewish and anti-Zionist feeling. I do not see how this can be doubted, yet cowardice, willed blindness and self-delusion are the most prominent reactions in the Jewish community at present. I have just come across a representative sample of this self-destructive attitude in the *guardian.co.uk* website for December 4, 2008. *Tikun Olam* blogger Richard Silverstein, a "good Jew" *par excellence*, opines that the Mumbai terrorists were "seeking redress for crimes against Palestine" and were the victims of "the Western jihad against radical Islam," of which Israel, naturally, is in the forefront. Note that in Silverstein's formulation the "jihad" is not conducted by radical Muslims but by the West, which for this commentator means essentially the United States and Israel.

Far too many Jews do not want to admit the obvious, preferring to dismiss those who are sounding the alarm as catastrophists or paranoiacs and proceeding with business as usual. And business as usual means not only going on as if nothing untoward is occurring but actually collaborating, whether through deliberate ignorance or programmatic hospitality, with those who harbour ill will against the Jewish people. We may even posit another category of business as usual which for most other peoples would be considered highly unusual. I refer to that subclass of Jews, mentioned above, who have made common cause with their enemies, defamers and traducers—prominent anti-Zionists like Noam Chomsky, Norman Finkelstein, Alfred Grosser, Naomi Klein, Tony Judt, Jaqueline Rose, Avi Shlaim, Moshe Machover, Haim Bresheeth and Richard Falk, whose hatred of Israel is so extreme and untextured as to be scarcely distinguishable from antisemitism. Such apostates do not scruple to trade in apocrypha when indulging their animus against their own people, even when they can be readily exposed.

The example of Jacqueline Rose is a salient one in this respect. Reputable scholars like Walter Laqueur (*TLS*, April 21, 2006), Paul

Bogdanor (*FrontPageMagazine*, September 4, 2006) and Alvin Rosenfeld (*American Jewish Committee*, December 2006) have exposed Rose's attempt in her *The Question of Zionism* to establish an ideological kinship between Adolf Hitler and the founder of Zionism, Theodor Herzl, by placing them in the same Paris audience attending a performance of Wagner's *Lohengrin* in 1895. Apart from the fact that this would prove nothing anyway, Hitler, who was born in 1889 and would have been only six years old at the time, did not enter Paris until 1940 with the conquering German army. (As Bogdanor later pointed out in an article for *Zeek* online, April 2007, the offending matter was dropped from the paperback edition of Rose's book.) The trouble is that such Jewish anti-Zionist propagandists, who traffic in all kinds of outright distortion, are by no means in short supply and their names are practically interchangeable. A Rose by any other name would smell as foul.

But if we do not court a comfortable state of oblivion to what is transpiring everywhere around us, we can sense the rising swell of predatory anticipation in a world preparing to cast out its chosen scapegoat from the body of nations. One of Israel's very few Muslim friends, who has the interests of Jews and Israelis at heart, has stated this clearly. Sheikh Abdul Hadi Palazzi, Director of the Cultural Institute of the Italian Islamic Community, despairs of Israel's future. "The nations of the world," he predicts, are "once again preparing bad days for the Jewish people" (*IsraelNationalNews.com*, December 21, 2007). He may well be right. What we may be observing all around us are the preliminary signs and stages of a world readying itself to launch the next Holocaust: Ever Again.

Once more, George Steiner is as penetrating as he is provocative: "Somewhere the determination to kill Jews, to harass them from the earth simply because they *are*, is always alive." At the end of the day, it really is that simple. And the end of the day, let us also remember, is the beginning of the night.[17]

Notes

[1] "The hatred for Judaism," says Freud in *Moses and Monotheism*, "is at bottom hatred for Christianity," a religion deriving from Judaism and forced upon a civilization which has remained "barbarically polytheistic." The Christian's self-hatred is thus projected upon his source and proxy. At the same time, public sentiment, ideological analysis, political theory and official policy work hand in hand toward the disintegration of a grand historic enterprise designated as "the West.

[2] David Horowitz warns in an interview in the *Western Standard* (November 2006): "The left is larger than it's ever been and much more dangerous, in part because of the alliance with Islamofascism that it's made. It's captured the schools…Our universities are now like Third World universities. They've been politicized. They've been subordinated to leftist agendas. They indoctrinate students." And the primary victim of this noxious ideological package is, naturally, Israel. As Pascal Bruckner explains, "The more one moves leftward on the political spectrum, the more virulent are the attacks against Israel. This is because the Left has fastened its anti-Western principles onto the Hebrew state." From the standpoint of this leftist version of antisemitism, "Israel incarnates all the obscenity of the West, the more so because it is located in the land of the East!" Ultimately, as Westerners who have fallen into a condition of "uncertainty and softness" and who no longer have "the will to fight and assert" themselves, we need to be reminded that "Israel must be recognized as our own past and a still-living call to resistance." But our own past is precisely what we are ashamed of, although, on balance, we have probably done at least as much good as harm. Recently, I found myself in a taxi driven by a Haitian immigrant. In the course of our conversation about the "troubles" in his home country, I asked him what solution he might propose for so violent and recidivist a state of affairs. "We must be occupied again," he replied, "by a new colonial administration. The West must reconquer us. There is no other solution." The distinguished intellectual historian Paul Johnson feels

the same way; he has advocated the "recolonization" of most of Africa (*New York Times Magazine*, April 18, 1993).

[3] This is the same Jimmy Carter who is noted for befriending many of the world's dictators, including Kim Il Sung ("I find him to be vigorous, intelligent…"), Nicolae Ceausescu ("We believe in enhancing human rights"), Hafez Assad ("I find him to be constructive in attitude"), Josip Broz Tito, Fidel Castro, Raul Cedras, Robert Mugabe (it was Carter's meddling in the internal affairs of Rhodesia that led to the installation of the Mugabe regime in what is now Zimbabwe) and, of course, arch-terrorist Yasser Arafat, one of whose speeches framed "for Western ears," according to Carter's biographer Douglas Brinkley, the former President helped draft. Carter's legacy persists today in the Iranian fiasco. Kenneth Stein, who resigned from the Carter Center in protest over the publication of *Palestine Peace Not Apartheid*, wrote in the *Middle East Quarterly* (Spring 2007) that Carter "does what no non-fiction author should ever do: He allows ideology or opinion to get in the way of facts…To suit his desired ends, he manipulates information, redefines facts, and exaggerates conclusions…By adopting so completely the Palestinian historical narrative, Carter may hamper diplomatic efforts…that attempt to compel the Palestinian leadership to accept accountability for its actions." And as David Pryce-Jones writes in *Betrayal: France, the Arabs and the Jews*, "Carter's equivocating and inept zigzag of policy towards Iran had set the seal on a revolution with repercussions for the world as perilous as any of the great revolutions of history." For Arthur Schlesinger Jr. in his newly published *Journals 1952-2000*, "The election of Carter was a disaster to both the party and the country."

Carter has received new support from an unlikely source. Responding to a boycott petition signed by 16,000 pro-Palestinian customers, the Canadian online bookstore, Amazon.ca, buried a long negative review to which they objected, listed recently purchased books of such Israel-bashers as Ilan Pappe, Robert Fisk, Noam Chomsky and Norman Finkelstein, featured a fawning interview with the former President followed by an innocuous summary from *Booklist*, and posted nine reviews, six of which were overwhelmingly favourable and another taking exception only to the physical format of the book. Its American parent, Amazon.com, to its credit retained the objectionable review, but otherwise differed little in its presentation.

Reading Carter, whose writing has clearly deteriorated over the years, I am put in mind of that couplet from Byron's *Don Juan*:

In youth I wrote because my mind was full,
And now because I find it growing dull.

Although, frankly speaking, I am not sure the first line is wholly accurate.

[4] The Iranian threat has been consistently underestimated by the media. A typical instance is the CBC's *Fifth Estate* program whose installment, aired on March 7, 2007, focused on the Iraq "quagmire" to impugn the credentials of the administration of George W. Bush and, by implication, to treat the Iranian situation as a pretext for American warmongering. Such blind innocence founded in *schadenfreude* is ultimately lethal. A nuclear Iran in the hands of the Ayatollahs will change the world irrevocably. It is, of course, not only the media who are hiding their heads in the sand, but the intellectual mediocracy as well, having once again betrayed its fiduciary duties. One of the latter's most acclaimed exemplars is Slovenian cultural theorist Slavoj Zizek, now Director of the Birbeck Institute at the University of London. In an article for the webzine *In These Times*, entitled "Give Iranian Nukes a Chance," Zizek considers that Iran has a right to nuclear defense against "the global hegemony of the United States," denounces "the false premises of today's 'war on terror'," and believes that the logic of MAD would work to deter an Iranian nuclear strike against Israel. That the Iranian mullahs have already conducted a cost-benefit analysis of such an attack, arriving at the conclusion that forty million Iranian "martyrs" is a small price to pay for the obliteration of Israel, and are developing missiles capable of targeting all the major European cities, are facts of no account for the learned professor. That he also regards Iran as an "Arab state" should alert us to the extent of his ignorance.

[5] As Mark Twain wrote in *The Innocents Abroad*, "If these Arabs be like the other Arabs, their love for their beautiful mares is a fraud. Those of my acquaintance have no love for their horses, no sentiment

of pity for them, and no knowledge of how to treat them or care for them." His conclusion: "weep for the sentiment that has been wasted upon the Selims of romance." It is no great stretch, I fear, to extrapolate to the present and apply Twain's observations to the current Palestinian attempt to mount a State, let alone to care for it.

This is not meant as an insult. There is every objective indication that a self-divisive and volatile Palestinian state could only survive on international life-support if it were not to flatline in record time. Indeed, Palestine may one day *look like* a state, but it is doubtful that it would ever be anything more than a political hologram, a three-dimensional projection produced by a two-dimensional strip of paper. Chief negotiator Saeb Erekat makes loud noises about the Palestinians being ready for the "end game," but I am afraid there will be no dancing in the end zone for his people. They will fumble the ball on the way in, as they have repeatedly since the time of the Peel Commission. The Palestinians, like the Arabs in general, suffer from many ailments and afflictions, not the least of which is what the poet John Dryden, in *The Hind and the Panther*, called "the jaundice in the soul," envy—of Israeli accomplishments in farming, technology, medicine, education and the advancement of political freedoms. And as I have noted in text, small, local events have large, analogic significance. Following prayers at the Temple Mount, a crowd of 150 Arab-Israelis, protesting the Israeli excavations to repair a collapsed walkway in the area and shouting *Allahu Akbar*, pelted their own buses sent to take them home. One gets the impression that if Palestine were ever to become a state, it would be the largest insane asylum in the world.

But insanity is not an exclusively Palestinian prerogative. There is plenty of it to go around in Israel too, typified by the proposal of Shlomo Avineri, a leftist professor at Hebrew University, which envisages not a Western or international trusteeship for Palestine but a Saudi Protectorate. Avineri is correct when he recognizes that the structure of Palestinian society lacks "the basic ingredients of tolerance, legitimized pluralism and the understanding that differences are not to be decided by force and coercion." The proliferation of Palestinian militias and clan gangs make the possibility of a "functioning body politic totally unrealistic." But his conclusion is no less unrealistic; it is, not to put too fine a point on it, entirely demented. A Saudi Protectorate would bring the Wahabbi terrorist machine immediately adjacent to Israel's borders and create a far more alarming situation than what exists today. Nor are tolerance, pluralism and the peaceful reconciliation of difference mainstays of the Saudi regime. Nevertheless, despite the political lunacy of the previous Kadima Israeli leadership and the moral and intellectual delirium of the Israeli left-oriented professoriate and "Peace" movements, there are still enough brave and resourceful Israelis to provide some hope for the country's continued survival and prosperity.

[6] This was written some time before the eruption of full-scale civil war in Gaza; on June 13, 2007, a Palestinian journalist, speaking to *The Jerusalem Post*, offered confirmation: "The two state solution has finally worked," he said with bitter irony.

[7] Another treatise which seeks to dispel the manifold delusions of Western intellectuals and public opinion regarding the Israel-Palestine embruement is Mitchell Bard's *Myths and Facts*, which I cannot recommend highly enough. See also D.H.K. Amiran, "A letter from Palestine," in the *Geographical Review* (29), R. Kark, R. Aaronsohn and Z. Shillony, *Land Ownership and Settlement in Palestine 1800-1948*, and D. Gavish and J. Biger, "Innovative Cartography in Palestine, 1917-1918," in *The Cartographical Journal* (159), among many other such studies. The name "Palestina" is a first century A.D. Roman coinage and was revived only with the British Mandate. As for the millions of Palestinians we hear about daily in the press, they are by no means descendants of an original population native to the area in question and, indeed, did not come to consider themselves "Palestinians" until the interlude between the 1967 war and the 1974 Rabat Conference. As Stephen Schecter makes clear in an article for the *Think-Israel* website, the Arabs and "Palestinians" have turned history inside out, claiming that "the Jews have no connection to Jerusalem, that the Jews who inhabited ancient Israel were not Jews, and that the Second Temple destroyed by the Romans did not exist." While the West has, for the most part, refused to accept such arrant nonsense, it has bought into the lie of Palestinian proprietorship wholesale.

[8] As former terrorist recruit Ed Husain wrote in the *Telegraph.co.uk* for May 2, 2007, "To argue that dialogue will win over extremist Islamists is a myth; theirs is a mindset that is not receptive to alternative views." The notion of "dialogue" is, as often as not, only another convenient smokescreen, cliché or piece of self-deception. Tariq Ramadan, to take a well-known example, is a strong advocate of "dialogue," in particular between Islam and the West. In a talk given at Queens' College, Cambridge on June 14, 2006 in which he promoted the value of "dialogue," he was visibly taken aback by a question posed by the noted historian of Islamic thought, Dr. Eric Ormsby. Ormsby wanted to know why, if peaceful discussion between adversaries offered the best hope of reconciliation, there was no dialogue between the warring Sunni and Shi'a branches of Islam. Taken aback, Ramadan, a Sunni Muslim, at first replied, "I don't know," then bethought himself and pointed to Shi'a recalcitrance: "It is because they insulted the Companions of the Prophet." *Ipse dixit*.

[9] See Shlomo Riskin's *Torah Lights* for a development of this theme. David Mamet in *The Wicked Son* is acidly contemptuous of the of the American left-wing Israel-bashing Jew, whom he calls the *apikoros*, the Yiddish/Hebrew word for skeptic, atheist or apostate. "Who are these vile friends on the Left," he asks, "who enjoy and applaud themselves for enjoying the quirks, customs, and observances of every race and culture but their own? They are a plague." He accuses these Jews of "preemptive treason," that is, "selling out, in advance, their own."

[10] Even the Vatican, in its 1965 Nostra Aetate Declaration, proclaimed by Pope Paul VI, put an end to such acts of slander, effectively ending the cult of Saint Simonio, the Christian child alleged to have been sacrificed in Trent. We may never get to see the original pages which Toaff has rewritten and so we are obliged to be circumspect in order not to embark on a witch hunt. But comments in the press by those who have read the pre-edited version and the very fact that Toaff considered it necessary to halt publication and make changes to the text constitute a form of circumstantial evidence. It is legitimate to speculate whether Toaff's pre-revised pages would have been reminiscent of John Harvey's Penguin history of the Plantagenets,

which tried to draw suspicion upon the Jewish community of 12th and 13th century England. "Whatever we may think of the evidence in favour of 'ritual murder,' " Harvey writes, "a number of instances of mysterious child-murder undoubtedly did occur," which in his estimation justified the wholesale expulsion of Jews from England. Harvey also cites Chaucer's "Prioress's Tale" (as if a literary text constitutes judicial evidence) which tells the story of an "innocent child" murdered by Jews and which also cites Hugh of Lincoln—or Little Saint Hugh—"likewise murdered so/By cursed Jews." "Murder will out," writes Chaucer; but slander and defamation, it seems, especially when it comes to Jews, are always in. One recalls the influential French diplomat and scholar Louis Massignon who argued that the blood libel was an attested historical fact. Harvey and Massignon commit a sin of scholarship; Toaff, as a Jew, may be doubly compromised, even if his intentions were not motivated by an ulterior design.

[11] A Prime Minister (Olmert) who seriously considered a Saudi peace plan which envisages the cession of Judea, Samaria, the Jordan Valley, East Jerusalem and the Golan Heights, as well as implementing a symbolic (whatever this may mean) "right of return" of hostile Arabs to Israeli land; a Chief of Staff (Halutz) who sold off his stock portfolio in the middle of a war; and a Minister of Defense (Peretz) who peered at Hizbullah emplacements through capped binoculars and refused to act when missiles were raining down upon southern Israel and even upon his own home town—these do not inspire much in the way of confidence, or anything else, for the future of the country. One may be gratified that the fate of the three rebels who "rose up" before Moses in *Numbers* 16 was transposed electorally to the present situation and that the Israeli populace threw the bums out. Foreign Minister Tzipi Livni does not figure in this Biblical analogy, but it is clear that she too had to go, as she is part of the same family.

One would like to believe that Jews can survive their enemies, but can they resist the passion for self-decimation? The Soncino Gesselschaft Pentateuch of 1933 which Hitler prevented from being completed still exists as a testament to dogged longevity in the midst of tragic circumstances. But another text, the recent Soda-Club commercial published in Israeli newspapers, which promises a seltzer and soda maker that produces "an endless supply of the freshest, fizziest seltzer—all at the touch of a button, with no clean-up," is an alarming danger signal in the growing shadow of possible nuclear annihilation at the touch of a button with no clean-up. It is not only Israelis who should be worried; Jews of the Diaspora are equally implicated. I know in my bones that if Israel goes, they'll be coming for me next. And all the Jew can reasonably expect from the liberal world in which he has invested his loyalty is a candlelight vigil.

[12] As *Jerusalem Post* correspondent Caroline Glick notes (January 23, 2007), in an article reporting on the Dromi affair: "Iska Leibowitz, the chief prosecutor in the southern district, is the daughter of the late professor Yeshayahu Leibowitz, one of the ideological founders of the radical left in Israel and the earliest prominent Israeli purveyor of the obscene comparison between Israel and Nazi Germany. Her nephew, attorney Shamai Leibowitz, is a radical anti-Zionist attorney." The latter defended the notorious terrorist Marwan Barghouti and has been active in seeking for American divestment from Israel. The Israeli juristocracy has in large measure become an enemy of the state. Recently, however, the law against shooting at burglars and assailants has been revoked, allowing farmers to protect themselves in the absence of adequate policing.

[13] With respect to the political left, one thinks of that old Jewish joke. What is the best way to get to heaven? Turn right and go straight.

[14] George Jonas suggests in *Beethoven's Mask* that "Well-meaning efforts to stamp out anti-Semitism, along with other forms of ethnic and racial prejudice, might be misplaced. By targeting prejudice, perhaps we have got hold of the wrong end of the stick…People who dislike Jews are not the big problem. The big problem is people who think it right to blow up people they dislike." But of course, antisemitism lends itself especially to strengthening the tendency toward detonation.

[15] Here at home, acclaimed leftist historian Roger Morris (*Globe and Mail*, November 18, 2006) pummeled the U.S. for its "bond of ignorance" in the "post-Holocaust *laissez-passer* granted Israel" and

attacked President Bush for his "myopic, self-defeating collusion with Israel." But the degree to which Morris can be trusted as a viable historian is attested by his use of a mythological metaphor, referring to "the Ariadne's thread of preconception, arrogance and deception…that mark governments bent on policies at odds with their own interests." Ariadne's thread, of course, leads *from* the labyrinth *to* salvation, not the other way around.

[16] The world's morbid attention is turned almost exclusively toward Israel, a comparatively innocent state in the gladiatorial arena of international devastations. Meanwhile anti-Mugabe demonstrators in Zimbabwe are regularly beaten, imprisoned, tortured and killed. There were a million marchers in London to protest the Iraq war which led to the capture of the world's greatest mass murderer since Hitler, Stalin, Mao and Pol Pot. How many of this million organized or participated in public demonstrations in sympathy with the oppressed and brutalized Zimbabweans? Where are the million peace marchers protesting the unspeakable events in Darfur? How many noble souls can we count demonstrating in the streets against China's treatment of the Falun Gong? Why is no one proposing to boycott and divest from Zimbabwe, Sudan, China, Syria, Iran, Cuba, Venezuela, Russia, Egypt, Saudi Arabia and other notable violators of the most elementary human rights—not excluding Palestine itself? The question, of course, is rhetorical.

[17] The Jew simply cannot win. If he is not condemned for representing himself as "first-born, favourite child of God the Father" (to cite Freud's words from *Moses and Monotheism*), setting himself apart from the Gentile, then he is blamed for implanting the idea of Chosenness in the Gentile psyche, as Arnold Toynbee believed. The trap cannot be sprung. Equally distressing, as I have been at pains to point out, is the Jewish tendency to self-destructiveness. If the *pinteleh Yid*, the presumably eternal spark of Jewishness, is ever to be extinguished, it will be as much at the hands of the JINOs (Jews In Name Only) and *yordim* (the "fallen community") as at the hands of their enemies.